DEEP SLEEP STORIES FOR STRESS RELIEF

Bedtime Lullabies for Stressed-Out Adults. How to Improve Your Relaxation and Fall Asleep Faster with Meditation Tales to Revitalize Your Body and Life.

© **Copyright 2019 - All rights reserved.**

The content contained within this book may not be reproduced, duplicated, or transmitted without direct written permission from the author or the publisher.

Under no circumstances will any blame or legal responsibility be held against the publisher, or author, for any damages, reparation, or monetary loss due to the information contained within this book. Either directly or indirectly.

Legal Notice:

This book is copyright protected. This book is only for personal use. You cannot amend, distribute, sell, use, quote or paraphrase any part, or the content within this book, without the consent of the author or publisher.

Disclaimer Notice:

Please note the information contained within this document is for educational and entertainment purposes only. All effort has been executed to present accurate, up to date, and reliable, complete information. No warranties of any kind are declared or implied. Readers acknowledge that the author is not engaging in the rendering of legal, financial, medical, or professional advice. The content within this book has been derived from various sources. Please consult a licensed professional before attempting any techniques outlined in this book.

By reading this document, the reader agrees that under no circumstances is the author responsible for any losses, direct or indirect, which are incurred as a result of the use of the information contained within this document, including, but not limited to, — errors, omissions, or inaccuracies.

Table of Contents

INTRODUCTION 1

CHAPTER ONE WHAT IS SELF HYPNOSIS? 10

CHAPTER TWO: STORIES OF THE SIBERIA 51
    NORTHERN LIGHTS 51
    NOMADIC PASTORALS 53
    REINDEERS 55
    SLED 59
    POLAR BEAR 62
    SEALS 65

CHAPTER THREE: STORIES OF THE JUNGLE 66
    TROPICAL RAIN FOREST 66
    RIVERS 69
    PARROTS ECHOED 71
    BIG TREES 74
    TRIBU 76
    MONKEYS 79

CHAPTER FOUR: STORIES OF TROPICAL ISLANDS 82
    ATOLLO 82
    MY SUMMER WITH PALMS 85
    THE BLUE OCEAN 87

CHAPTER FIVE: OTHER STORIES 89
    THREE SIMPLE RULES 89
    THE ARROGANT SWANS 91
    THE IGNORANT MAN 92
    GRACE AND LOLA 94
    THE CLEVER EUNICE 104

CHAPTER 6: STORIES OF THE COUNTRYSIDE 107
    JOSH AND BUDDY, THE FLUPPY PUPPY 107
    THE PURPLE ALOE 110
    ZACH, THE FOGGILY DUCK 113
    THE STORY OF FORTE THE CAT. 116
    THE STORY OF THE GREAT IROKO TREE 119
    THE GRASS STORY 122
CONCLUSION 125

Introduction

Stress has fast become an essential part of our daily lives. A typical stressful day usually involves interactions with children, a spouse, employees, a nagging boss, and other communications. In addition to this stressful mix, there are daily worries that can rob life of peace and harmony. These concerns include paying bills, broken cars, mortgages, health issues, etc.

The outside world too quickly puts us under emotional, mental, and physical pressure. The older we get, the more serious the effects of stress on the mind and body can be, and too much can lead to hormonal imbalances that make a person anxious and overactive. The key to relieving stress and anxiety naturally would be downtime and healthy habits.

If you are looking for stress relief, you may be frustrated with the number of suggestions available. Everyone seems to have a way to reduce these subtle but powerful influences that not only ruin our joie de vivre but can also often cause mental health problems that go far beyond the original cause of the problem.

There are many options available to manage your daily life better. Some of these options include meditation, yoga, hobbies, etc. and while most of the information you receive on stress relief is valid, you should spend time testing the ideas and figuring out what kind of stress reliever is right for you and your situation.

Current scientific studies show that sleep is one of the most critical factors for stress relief. It's an area you cannot cheat. You need to have enough rest every day to live a long, healthy life. It's the best way to have enough energy every day to fight stress, and one prominent way that stress shows up is in sleep schedules. When you are stressed, you usually find it challenging to fall asleep at night. As a rule, 8 hours of sleep should be enough for a healthy adult.

Here are a couple of ways you can calm down at night and get some good sleep.

INTRODUCTION

Choose a schedule and stick to it.

Choose a time to fall asleep and a time to get up. Keep this up every day, including the days when you have the privilege of sleeping. Sleeping only 1-2 days a week can disrupt your sleep schedule for the entire week. If you lie down and are not tired, do not get up. Read a book or listen to music to relax.

Avoid Caffeine - Reduce Caffeine (even if you think it won't affect you) at least 6 hours before going to sleep.

Smoking - If you smoke, avoid smoking an hour before bed. Smoking can cause restless sleep.

Create a relaxing routine - take a bath or shower, read a book, listen to soothing music, or stretch before bed to relax your body and mind.

Avoid snacks until late at night - Reduce snacks after dinner to simple and easily digestible meals. When the body works to digest a lot of food, it can disrupt the sleep process. Avoid snacks with artificial additives or sweeteners and avoid protein.

Prepare for the night - Prepare for the next day as much as possible. Get dressed. Plan your day. Preparation helps you relax and sleep better.

Create a sleep-friendly environment: If you find it difficult to fall asleep at night, take a look at your room. Is it overloaded, ruffled, disorganized, or overly decorated with many items? Being able to fall asleep at night can be as easy as cleaning your room! Our outer environment often reflects our inner state of being. If we keep our spaces organized, we have an area where we can relax and not be disturbed by the chaos of the day or by our mind.

Make the room as dark as possible - use an eye mask if necessary. Use earplugs to block the sound, or use a fan or soft music to mask the sounds that can interfere with sleep. Turn your watch, so you don't see the time. All of these tips will help make a relaxing atmosphere for you to sleep in.

Maintain a consistent bedtime routine - For those of you who have children, you can understand this mantra. A regular bedtime is essential for babies to learn to sleep through the night, but it is also vital for adults. By following a routine, we create a physiological response in our body that prepares us for sleep. If we end our evening the same way every night, our body begins to suspect what will follow, which is ultimately sleep. Routines don't have to be elaborate or complicated to be effective. It should consist of things that calm and relaxes you and leave you with good thoughts and feelings.

Listen to music explicitly made for sleeping - Listening to profoundly soothing and melodic music and inviting your mind to let go of raging thoughts is perfect for relaxing at the end of a busy day. When music is used as part of your bedtime, it puts you in a state where sleep is the next and most natural response. Repeating music can also help you sleep overnight, creating a deep refreshing sleep.

With the push of a button, you can fill your home or office with fantastic music that works behind the scenes to reduce the pressure you feel during the day. Then you can use the same music to put yourself into a sweet and restful sleep. Relaxation music requires very little preparation, is very inexpensive, and offers you a level of anxiety and stress relief that you have never experienced before!

If you have trouble sleeping, you can also follow these additional tips:

- Turn off the electronics and turn your watch away from you (don't look at the clock or check your phone if you can't sleep). Don't worry if you can't fall asleep, and remember that your body will eventually take control and help you relax.

- If you are awake in bed for more than 20 minutes, move to another part of the house (one without a bright light). Do something relaxing for a while until you feel tired and go back to bed.

HOW TO BEAT STRESS

Here are some stress relief ideas that are simple, cheap, and sometimes even free:

1. Always take time out.

Stressful situations often compound our lives, and we must take a 10-minute break to relax during the day. For example, on a hectic day, take 10 minutes to relieve stress, such as deep breathing and stretching.

2. Go outside to recharge your batteries.

Don't stay locked in the house or office all day, as this will make you darker and more anxious. You need to get enough sunshine every day as this is important to increase serotonin production in the body and thereby increase mood and energy.

3. Exercise regularly.

Movement is essential for the human body to function effectively. It eliminates toxins from the body (such as lactic acid and uric acid, which are partly responsible for stress). It is a natural remedy to relieve stress and anxiety as it increases endorphins, reduces stress, optimizes physical performance, and sharpens the mind. You don't have to do any strenuous activities. Something as simple as a 30-minute brisk walk paired with deep breathing every day will work wonders to relieve stress.

4. Have a favorite relaxation ritual.

A fun way to relieve stress is to wait for something relaxing and rewarding at the beginning or end of the day. Here are some suggestions for natural relief from stress and anxiety:

- Have a soothing drink. Herbal or green tea and hot milk with cinnamon and honey are popular favorites.

- Stretch yourself while using the shower to release tension.

- Write in a diary to relax before bed. Knowing your thoughts, problems, and arousal can clear and calm your mind so you can fall asleep fairly quickly.

5. Another approach to relieving anxiety is to join an organized group that can help you relax. This group activity allows you to make contacts and reduce anxiety and stress. The downside, however, is that you have to take the time to attend classes. All good intentions in the world are useless if you don't find the time to introduce yourself!

One of the best ways to relieve anxiety and stress is to integrate all of these approaches into your current lifestyle seamlessly. These activities provide a soothing and relaxing sensory contribution to stress relief and can be done by almost everyone according to their lifestyle and preferences.

It is possible to reduce stress.

1. To relieve stress, you need to learn to deal with incidents, situations, and stressful people. If you are too busy in the office, you will learn to reject tasks that you think you cannot do. You have to learn to say no because if you accept things that you cannot do, you have a problem that will strain you. If some people bother you too, avoid them.

2. Calm your mind. Plan time in a day to do something you enjoy. For example, if you like to work in the garden, you can do this for half an hour in the morning before preparing to work. If you want to watch a movie, you can do it before bed. Focus on them during these activities, and do not think about other things that worry you.

3. Calm your body. You can do this by getting an hour of massage. Use an aroma oil with lavender scent or rose petals to apply it to your body as this will help relieve tension and relax your body. You can also take a hot bath at night before bed, as hot water relieves tense muscles. Take a dip in your bathtub and pour drops of aromatherapy body wash or oil into the water.

4. Eat well. If you do not eat a balanced diet, your body will weaken, and the need for stress relief will increase. You need a few reserves to deal with the onslaught of stress. Make sure you eat lots of fruits and vegetables and include lean meats and fish in your diet. Avoid sweets and fortified foods with low nutritional value.

MEDITATION

Meditation is a simple technique that, when practiced for only 10 minutes a day, can help you control stress, reduce anxiety, improve cardiovascular health, and achieve a more exceptional ability to relax. Research has shown that meditation, including mindfulness meditation, can offer significant health benefits that have virtually no disadvantages. Not only is it useful for dealing with stress, but studies have also shown that it can also help fight insomnia.

When our body suddenly experiences stress or a threat, we respond with a characteristic "fight or flight" reaction. The "adrenaline rush" we experience is the result of the release of the hormones adrenaline (adrenaline) and noradrenaline. They cause an increase in blood pressure and pulse, faster breathing, and increased blood flow to the muscles. This function gives us the space to find out what our valid energy, attention, and emotions require, which are

INTRODUCTION

legitimate and which are not. Think about it: if we could distinguish the two, our experience of stress and anxiety would be very different. We feel pressure when we don't have this space in our thoughts and our life. We feel relieved when meditation gives us space and clarity we need to organize our priorities. One standard vehicle for reflection is breathing exercises.

- Deep breathing: One of the easiest ways to relax is to control your breathing. Only ten deep breaths can have a positive effect, and more intensive breathing exercises are available for more relaxation. Close your eyes and notice your breathing. Pay close attention to your natural breathing frequency and feel how the air flows in and out of your nose or mouth. Imagine the flow of air that flows through the mouth, airways, abdomen, and outwards. Examine your body for tension. When you exhale, you feel the stress leave this part of your body. Imagine how your breathing reaches your forehead, neck, shoulders, arms, and then release the tension after the end.

- Guided imagery. This exercise helps you to focus your attention on an image or story so that your mind can let go of the worries or thoughts that keep you awake. Get a comfortable position in bed. Close your eyes and relax. Start visualizing a scene, memory, or story that you find comforting. It's very individual - find what works best for you by trying a few options. A few examples are a favorite vacation or a peaceful place outdoors, a relaxing activity like cuddling up with a book in your favorite chair, or something repetitive like remembering steps from an exercise or a dance routine.

- The key is to find something to focus your attention on and let go of other thoughts. Create this scenario in your head. Visualize all details of the picture or story as slowly and carefully as possible. Whenever you find that your mind wanders (a worry for the day or a "must" for tomorrow), recognize it and let it go. Return to your relaxing story. It doesn't matter if it takes a while before it works. Every time you exercise, you will improve.

- Progressive muscle relaxation: This is a technique that stretches and relaxes muscles throughout the body in a specific order. It can help reduce mental and physical stress and can be beneficial before bed.

- Find the time to exercise: Daily training can help relieve stress and help you sleep well. This does not mean that you have to run a marathon. Even moderate exercise can be a boon to your mood and sleep, especially if it's constant. Exercise also offers many other benefits to other aspects of your health.

Consult a doctor or psychiatrist

If sleep disorders affect your daily life, it is essential to see a doctor who can make a thorough assessment to identify possible causes. Following the established diagnostic process can determine if there are more serious health problems that need treatment and can help the doctor learn the most appropriate treatment for your needs.

COMBATING STRESS-INDUCED INSOMNIA

There are countless ways to improve your sleep hygiene. Some notable examples are:

- Set up a consistent sleep schedule so that your body and your daily rhythm work to your advantage.

- Follow the same bedtime every night to relax mentally and physically while sleeping.

- Make your bed comfortable and supportive, and your bedroom free from excessive light or outside noise that could be disturbing.

- Minimize the use of electronic devices, including cell phones, in the hour before bedtime, as they create mental stimulation and emit blue light that can suppress the body's production of melatonin, a sleep-promoting hormone.

- Journaling - If you wake up at night because you can't stop thinking about something that causes you to stress during the day, journaling can be a useful technique for you. It can help you clear your mind, deal with strong emotions that make you lose sleep, think about things, and develop plans that can help you deal with situations that are stressful for you.

- Work through your stress - If you lose sleep due to anxiety, you may be able to relax and sleep better by changing your perspective. Anxiety, including the type that keeps you awake at night, is often a natural response to situations that require some kind of action. If you see your status as a challenge rather than a threat, you can switch to an active decision-making mode instead of staying in a passive and anxious state.

It is also a good idea to use your bedroom mainly for sleeping, to connect your bed and bedroom to sleep rather than stress. Consider getting up and reading a book, doing things at home, and doing other non-stimulating activities that can promote sleep when you're ready. If you still find it difficult to fall asleep at night, do the following:

1. Try not to fall asleep when you go to bed.

Focus on relaxing and recuperating, knowing that sleep will follow. This will put less pressure on falling asleep and help you rest sooner rather than later.

2. Enjoy being in bed.

Stop worrying about the speed at which you fall asleep and enjoy the moment in bed, comfortable, calm, and without responsibility.

3. Take a hot bath or shower.

Recent research has shown that a warm bath or shower, preferably one to two hours before bed, can help people fall asleep faster - 36% more quickly, to be precise.

4. Use the hour before bed to meditate and relax.

It will help you take your time to meditate and relax on purpose. If you feel worst in either area, you should use an app or device to help you. Headspace offers endless possibilities for short and long meditations. It gradually helps you to meditate for an hour (or more if you dare).

5. Try to address your concerns.

Whether you're scared or just thinking about what to do the next day, it is sometimes easier to worry after your head hits the pillow than to relax.

6. Read a book.

Relaxing at the end of the day is essential if the goal is to fall asleep quickly. One way to do this is to read well. However, light, engaging non-fiction is probably the best way to relax. Otherwise, you may want to stay awake all night to find the end.

7. Focus on your breathing.

Stressed or anxious people suffer from chronic under-breathing because stressed people breathe shallowly and short and often even hold their breath unconsciously. To relax, work on breathing as you imagine a number in your head. While it sounds a little weird, it almost always helps you slow down and relax.

8. Change your sleeping arrangements.

Have you ever thought that you couldn't fall asleep because your body subconsciously thinks your bed is not comfortable? You may find that adding a pillow-top mattress, soft pillows, and cozy sheets is all you need to get to sleep.

9. Don't be afraid to lower the temperature.

The idea of lowering the temperature in your bedroom can be off-putting. However, according to Sleep Advisor, it is easier to fall asleep in somewhat more relaxed rooms.

Chapter One
What Is Self Hypnosis?

PART 1

Self-hypnosis is easy to learn and can significantly improve your quality of life. The benefits of an excellent hypnosis relaxation session reflect in your daily life and help you feel a lot calmer. Here's how:

1. Find a comfortable place to relax and sit or lie down and make sure that your arms and legs are not crossed and relaxed.

2. Concentrate on your breathing, take a deep breath, and let go of it slowly. Sometimes, when you inhale and exhale, it can help you relax.

3. In either case, you may want to close your eyes now or before. The next step is to relax your body. This step is essential because we know that you do to a relaxed body and an anxious mind at the same time. There are various techniques for body relaxation. I like to imagine a little ball of warm light (maybe the sun) floating in front of your forehead. You can then direct this warm light from your head to the tip of your toes around your body and imagine how it massages, calms, and relieves every part of the body down to every tiny cell during the process. The more specific you are, the more relaxed you become. For example, imagine how even your nails become more comfortable. If you encounter concerns during your relaxation time, acknowledge them, and let them float.

4. Then you can imagine being at the top of ten levels. You may have already planned what will greet you at the end of the steps. Make sure it's a beautiful place to be, so relaxed when you're there. Take the time to go through every step of your imagination. Give

yourself a positive statement for each level, such as "I am relaxing so profoundly now." Use your imagination to make this experience as vivid as possible. Switch on your five senses entirely.

5. When you have reached the last step, you can relax in the place you have imagined. It can be a lovely garden, a forest or a beautiful beach. Use your senses again to fully appreciate the sounds, feelings, smells, and sights unique to the location you selected.

6. Finally, return to the process. Imagine you descend each level, making pronouncements as you go. Do this until you are ready to open your eyes and continue your day feeling good.

How does hypnosis work to relieve stress? The hypnosis session consists of two main parts. One is deep relaxation, and the other is the planting of positive messages and images. The subconscious is exceptionally receptive to new programs in a deeply relaxed state. This state is called the "trance" state.

Positive words such as "my mind is calm and clear" or "my self-esteem is overflowing" or "my desire for nicotine is gone" can be printed on the subconscious. When the session is over, you leave the state of trance in a conscious state.

Self-hypnosis is easy, and with a little practice, you can let your imagination run wild and try different relaxation methods to see what works for you.

Are you stressed most of the time? If your worrying is a constant habit, you will be relieved of the stress with hypnosis and self-hypnosis. It takes a while to learn this skill, but once you learn it, you can change your life and become calm and confident no matter the circumstances.

You may know that hypnosis can help, but it can bother you a little. Stage hypnotists often give the impression that their subjects are under their control, which can alarm you because you don't want someone to have power over your mind.

While hypnosis is mind control, YOU are still in control, whether someone else hypnotizes you or you do it yourself. Hypnosis is only a moderate state of trance. It's like watching a movie that you're immersed in or dreaming. They don't fall asleep and always know what's going on. You can "wake up" at any time, as you do when you imagine.

Anxiety is a bad habit, so hypnosis reprograms your subconscious by planting suggestions. These suggestions will help your psyche, the "automatic" part of you, to find other ways to get what you want without causing fear. In a way, you have acquired the bad habit of fear through stress, so hypnosis reprograms your mind so that you can relax more quickly and solve your challenges. After a hypnosis session, you will be completely relaxed and comfortable and experience this comfort in your daily life.

You will feel the effects immediately. For example, if you are worried about work, you will find that you are more relaxed and that the situations that have strained you no longer affect you in this way.

To induce self-hypnosis means to self-induce deep relaxation.

For some people, this may be the first time that they experience deep relaxation. As you relax deeply, you are very impressive, so the suggestions the hypnotherapist gives you have a big impact.

Remember to ask the hypnotherapist for some tips on how to trigger self-hypnosis: Most therapists have CDs and tapes available for you to practice at home.

While hypnosis is beneficial in relieving stress, it can work wonders in all areas of your life, especially those that cause stress - for example, at work and in your relationships.

Once you know what hypnosis looks like, you can create a light trance and make suggestions. Unlike claims that take a long time to produce results or that don't work at all, the recommendations you make with self-hypnosis work because your subconscious mind takes them into account and puts them into action.

Make a list of what you can intentionally and deliberately do to improve your life; to help you achieve your goals. You will be amazed at how quickly you can achieve your goals if you have made suggestions to achieve them.

In addition to reducing stress, the benefits of hypnosis include:

- Eliminate self-destructive behaviors
- End dependencies

- Increase self-esteem

- Improved health and well-being

- Sharpen the mental focus

- Rejuvenation and increased energy

- Strengthening relationships

- Memory retrieval

But for the effectiveness and speed of results, little can achieve the power of self-hypnosis for coping with and treating stress. Hypnosis can create a pleasant, calm state that is so far removed from the stress that it is called a "state of grace."

Indeed, self-hypnosis provides a way to relieve stress entirely and, thanks to the post-hypnotic suggestion, provides a valuable means of dealing with stress and anxiety. When done correctly, it can give robust stress relief and treatment that goes well beyond the actual self-hypnosis sessions. And the fantastic thing is that practicing self-hypnosis doesn't have to take forever.

One thing is sure: the time and effort invested in learning and then practicing a form of self-hypnosis bring real rewards in terms of relief and stress management. It is a robust method that helps you deal with stress, and possibly the most effective stress reliever available.

If you are struggling with stress regularly, self-hypnosis - with proper nutrition and moderate exercise - is the best stress management and relief tool you can use.

The first significant advantage of using hypnosis to manage stress is simply the hypnosis itself. Hypnosis is like a mental and spiritual massage.

Another factor, and probably the most significant factor in stress hypnosis, is the ability to give up on things that are beyond our control. As soon as you can give up things that are beyond your control, your stress level will drop. Too often, people let themselves be emotionally invested in situations, and while this is usually not a bad thing, it can sometimes be overwhelming.

Another great advantage of hypnosis for stress is the ability to tolerate others. Sometimes there are negative people in our lives who bother us. When someone has an unbearable boss at work, they can be hypnotized to be comfortable with the way that person is and let go of the things that previously bothered them.

How does hypnosis change your attitude to stress?

The answer is the subconscious which controls how you feel. It is the most primitive and least developed part of our brain. An example of how the subconscious controls our feelings is how we watch scary movies. When we watch scary movies, we are aware that nothing will happen to us, and the events of the film do not affect our lives. But this makes no difference to your subconscious, and that is why your heart pounds and your neck sweats.

But the beautiful thing is that hypnosis can help you change your subconscious mind exactly how you want it. Hypnosis is an experience that enables a hundred people. And from this experience, it makes you feel different at any time of the day.

If you haven't always had the natural ability to get the best out of every good or bad situation, this kind of positive, relaxed attitude doesn't happen by chance. To overcome a tendency towards stress, irritability, anger, or fear, you must train your mind to react positively to every situation and develop a deeply rooted tendency to always see the glass half full and not half empty. This is done through hypnosis, a daily program of relaxation, positive suggestions, and visualization. Your "instinctive" response to challenges and problems depends on the type and quality of your conscious thinking.

If you usually think that life in general consists mainly of a series of worries and irritations, you will often be stressed and angry. You will also find that many of the realities of your life seem to confirm this view somehow and that people always seem to give you reasons, intentionally or unintentionally, to get upset.

Your subconscious mind reacts to the harmful nature of these common conscious thoughts and works hard to create and translate your living conditions and their corresponding influences into reality. In other words, if you are still consciously thinking that life is stressful, your subconscious mind will ensure that a stressful life is what you get.

The subconscious mind - which contains or has access to power, wisdom, and skills beyond human understanding - is nevertheless guided by the nature of the thoughts, images, and feelings it receives from consciousness. Your consciousness guides your light, and the entire power of your subconscious is used for any purpose - positive or negative - that your conscious mind suggests typically.

As a result of your conscious mind training to consistently send positive thoughts and mental images into your subconscious mind, you will find that your tendency to stress and negativity will disappear, with all of the resulting benefits for psychological and physical health.

As mentioned above, this can be achieved by sticking to one or two daily sessions of relaxation, positive visualization, and confirmation; in other words, self-hypnosis. Take at least 10 minutes at least once a day to relax mentally and physically and to feel comfortable in a quiet place, preferably on a bed or a large chair. Close your eyes and start breathing deeply and regularly. Then imagine all your muscles, start with your feet and then work your way up to your neck and face, relax and unwind. After a few minutes - with a little practice – you'll have a floating feeling - evoke an image of calm and serenity in your head, or visualize yourself in situations in which you usually are stressed but see yourself calm and positive.

Maintain this visualization - improve yourself again with practice - while breathing relatively slowly and regularly. Then start saying silently or verbally that "I'm calm, relaxed and at peace" or "Every day I'm more relaxed in every way." Repeat the confirmation slowly and deliberately for about 20 to 30 times while maintaining your relaxed breathing and visualization.

After about 10 minutes, return to mindfulness and continue with everything you did before. If you do this once or preferably twice a day after just a few days, you will find that the stress will decrease and you will feel healthier and less prone to worry or tension. After a few weeks, you will find that your attitude towards life has changed in general. You will feel much happier, have better relationships with others, and also realize that no problem is more important than you. Self-hypnosis for relaxation also increases mental clarity and allows you to think faster about practical solutions to deal with difficulties that arise.

MINDFULNESS

We have so far established that our perception of and response to situations are essential in dealing with stress. There are often diverse ways to respond to any situation we find ourselves in, and mindfulness gives us more options for our response.

Mindfulness protects us

First of all, attentive practice helps us to pay attention to the present moment, to control the current, repetitive, and unproductive thoughts that lead to stress. Mindfulness enables us to regulate ourselves.

For example, suppose you don't get an instant response to a relevant text you sent to your partner. You could worry about what happened, fear that he's gotten hurt, and then think about all the things that could have gone wrong.

Instead, change your reaction by paying attention to what is going on at the moment. Instead of delving into self-created thoughts and concerns, you may notice a desire for response and the resulting fear. However, you would not react to these thoughts or intensify them, but return to your work.

This practice of paying attention to our experiences is not the standard mode for most people. Instead, we spend much of our time responding to events and producing explanations, implications, and stories that often cause stress. If we pay attention, we can maintain a more direct experience of the action and nothing more.

Mindfulness relieves you of pressure

Another aspect of mindfulness is an attitude of curiosity and acceptance of everything that is going on. In our example, you can accept that there are several reasons for not getting a response to your text. You might be curious if your partner doesn't take the text as important as you do.

Mindfulness and an open attitude leads to a greater acceptance of what is happening, a better ability to tolerate stressful situations, and a decrease in reactivity and repetitive negative thinking

Mindfulness creates a new relationship with experiences

According to some psychologists, the basic conscious practices of intention, attention, and attitude lead to a fundamental change of perspective to "rethink."

Mindfulness enables us to identify with thoughts, emotions, and physical sensations as they arise, and to be with them rather than being controlled or defined by them. We recognize that "this worry is not me" or "these thoughts are not me," which promotes the ability to see a situation as it is.

This practice increases our confidence in our ability to deal with events so that we are not stressed by events that would previously be perceived as a threat.

Mindfulness Practices

Stopping is an easy way to practice mindfulness in the face of stress. If you find that something has triggered and you want to respond, do the following:

Slow your movements

Breathe

Observe: What do you feel in your body? What do you think? What other options are there?

Continue considering several options.

It helps to put a friendly attitude into practice and to accept your thoughts and feelings as they are. It also helps to arouse curiosity to explore the situation with new eyes and to open up new opportunities. With everything that arises, ask yourself: Is this okay? Can I try this? You can practice this in small moments and develop skills that will serve you well in more difficult "crises."

What happens in the brain during meditation?

More and more research is investigating what happens in the brain during and after meditation. This evidence continually shows that mindfulness practice changes the structure and function of parts of the brain that are associated with emotional control. This corresponds to the behavioral studies conducted with experienced meditators, with the results showing that the practice of mindfulness improves self-regulation of attention and emotions.

The influence of mindfulness on the brain

Respond to threats

The area of the brain associated with the threat response, the amygdala, is smaller in meditators. In comparison, the area of the brain related to thoughtful reactions - the prefrontal cortex - is larger. These changes indicate that mindfulness reduces reactive and scary results that increase stress.

Regulation of emotions

Another area of the brain that changes after mindfulness training is the hippocampus. This part of the brain involved in regulating emotions.

What is the evidence of mindfulness for stress relief?

New evidence suggests that mindfulness effectively relieves anxiety and stress.

A 2014 review by scientists explicitly addressing the effects of mindfulness on stress relief found that "of the 17 studies, 16 were positive changes in psychological or physiological outcomes related to anxiety and stress." Despite the limitations in some studies that included smaller samples or no control group, the authors conclude that "mindfulness-based stress reduction is a promising method for stress management.

A recent systematic review of the American Medical Association (JAMA) journal found that "meditation programs can result in a small to moderate reduction in several negative dimensions of psychological stress." Mindfulness meditation programs have a similar effect to antidepressants usually prescribed for anxiety. Other magazines published in the past two years have consistently reported that mindfulness meditation has a positive impact on anxiety and stress.

Here are the things mindfulness can do in helping you to deal with stress:

1. You become more aware of your thoughts. You can then step back and not take them literally. This way, your stress response is not primarily triggered.

2. You do not react to situations as others would, that is, spontaneously. Rather, you sit back, properly analyze the situation with your "wise mind" to find the best solution, and then respond appropriately. Mindfulness helps you with meditation exercises.

3. Mindfulness activates your "being" mentality, which is associated with relaxation.

4. You are more aware and sensitive to your body's needs. You may notice pain earlier and then take the appropriate or necessary actions.

5. You are more emotionally empathetic. This is because you now have a higher level of emotional intelligence. Hence, as you increase in emotional intelligence, your tendency to react in anger to situations is greatly reduced.

6. You are more caring to yourself and others as you grow in mindfulness. This compassionate mind calms you down and inhibits your reaction to stress.

Practicing mindfulness reduces brain activity in the amygdala, which is necessary for activating your stress response so that your background stress level is effectively reduced.

You can concentrate better. When you do your work more efficiently, you feel better, which reduces the response to stress. You are more likely to enter "the zone" or "river" as Mihaly Csikszentmihalyi calls it in psychology.

You can change your attitude towards stress. Instead of just seeing the negative effects of stress, mindfulness allows you to think differently about stress itself. Watching the increased pressure helps you recharge your batteries, has a positive impact on your mind and body.

Remember a challenge in your life that causes stress. A situation that you can now work with. Not one of the very big challenges you faced, but not so small that it doesn't cause stress. A 3 on a scale of 1 to 10 is a good guide.

Remember the situation. Imagine yourself in the situation and all of the difficulties involved.

Notice if you can feel the stress in your body. Physical tension, faster heart rate, a little sweat, butterflies in the stomach, tension in the back or the shoulders or in the jaw, maybe. Pay attention to your stress signals.

Prepare yourself for your feelings. Notice how you feel. Label this emotion if you can, and pay close attention to where you feel the emotion in your body. Try to recognize it as much as possible. The more precisely you can localize the emotions, the more you'll notice the sensation, the better. With time and experience, you will continue to improve.

Bring conscious, attentive to emotions. This includes curiosity, friendliness, and acceptance.

Try to put your hand on the site of the sensation - a kind hand that represents kindness. Pretend to put your hand on a child's injured knee with care and affection.

Feel the feeling with your breath. This can promote awareness of the current moment and attitudes that are attentive to your experience.

When you are ready, stop this meditation

GUIDED MEDITATION

Guided meditation (sometimes referred to as guided image-guided meditation) is simply "meditation with the help of a guide." It is one of the easiest ways to get into a state of deep relaxation and inner silence and one of the most effective ways to reduce stress and bring about positive personal changes.

How does it look like?

Guided meditations happen when you let someone or something guide you while meditating. That person can be a meditation teacher or someone really experienced with meditation.

The first thing your meditation guide would do is to ask you to place your self in a comfortable sitting or lying position. You will then listen to your guide as he guides you through a series of relaxing visualizations. When you are relaxed and become calmer, the stress subsides, and your mind becomes clearer.

While in this deeply relaxed state of mind, your subconscious is open to positive suggestions, and your guide will use this time to take you on an inner journey that is meant to improve one or more aspects of your life. For example, guided meditation can be tailored to stress relief and insomnia reduction. It can also aim at healing you emotionally or developing you spiritually. You can join a guided tour to reach your full potential, or you can opt for a guided tour to experience deep relaxation.

As you can see now, guided meditation can be not only a relaxing experience but also one that improves your self-confidence, positively transforms your perspective, and inspires you to live your life to the fullest.

It is an effortless and enjoyable experience that leads to deep relaxation, stress relief, and increased esteem for life.

At the end of your meditation, your guide will gradually bring you back to a normal state of consciousness so that you feel refreshed, rejuvenated, and relaxed. A guided meditation can last from 5 minutes up to an hour, depending on personal preference. In most cases, guided meditation of 20 minutes or more is recommended if you want to experience a really deep state of relaxation and maximize the positive benefits.

What is the difference between guided meditation and traditional personal meditation?

Most traditional meditation techniques require that you take control of your own consciousness by focusing your attention on a single focus point. This focus could be your breathing, it could be a physical act, or more often, it could be a mantra - a tone, word, or phrase that you repeat mentally.

While these powerful meditation techniques are wonderful to achieve inner silence and improve your ability to concentrate, some people find it difficult to know fully.

Guided meditation has become so popularly preferred to traditional personal meditation techniques basically because they do not require prior training or effort to use them. Even if you are someone who finds it extremely hard to let go of your thoughts, even if you are very stressed or overwhelmed with mental activity, you will quickly find peace of mind if you are led rightly.

Because this type of meditation is so simple, it is beneficial for people who are new to meditation. However, guided meditations can also be very useful by people with a lot of meditation experience. Experienced meditators often use image-guided meditations to experience a deeper or more vivid meditation, to dive deeper into their minds than normal, or to address a particular aspect of personal development that they want to address.

Guided meditation is also quite different from traditional meditation in how it uses music and the sounds of nature to improve your meditation experience.

What do nature sounds and other kinds of music do in guided meditation?

Guided image meditation recordings usually include quiet meditation music that helps you relax as you are guided through the meditation. Think about the difference that a good soundtrack makes in a movie. Guided meditations benefit from music in the same way. Music adds another dimension of expression and depth to your guided meditation journey while calming your mind.

It is also not uncommon for CDs and MP3s with a guided meditation to contain sounds of nature. These sounds are very relaxing and can also be used to enhance the vividness of the visualizations you feel during meditation. For example, if you are led to visualize yourself on a sandy beach, your experience with this visualization will be more authentic if you can actually hear the sound of ocean waves.

In contrast to traditional meditation, in which your goal is to achieve mental calmness through concentration exercises, guided image meditations are based on a living tapestry of visualizations, music, and ambient sounds in order to relax and captivate you. Be careful and immerse yourself in an inner journey. Because this inner journey can be customized to achieve certain results, guided meditation can be even more powerful than traditional passive meditation techniques when it comes to making positive personal changes in your life.

Better Concentration - People who have actually learned to meditate and use guided meditation can continue to focus on the task at hand. You can relax completely and spend the rest of your day with a concentrated being. Guided meditation guides you through focusing on the meditation object, forcing the mind to focus on the goal, not the distractions that are usually present. By using guided meditation, even five or ten minutes a day, the mind gets a break from all the stresses that it endured. It leaves a feeling of peace.

Increase Energy - When you have finished your guided meditation, you should be relaxed and even refreshed. You will feel as if you can manage the rest of the day with confidence and look beyond the source of stress to find a good and reliable solution. Once you have reached the level of meditation guided by consciousness, you can do more and do what is necessary for yourself. You must train your mind from the distracted mind to a focused mind and then to the meditating mind to do this. It takes time to work your way through these three steps, but once you master them, it becomes easier to access the meditating mind.

<u>Reduce negative thoughts</u> - Guided mediation is a great way to improve yourself during the day and reduce the negative aspects of stress. It will only take a few minutes, and you will feel incredibly refreshed and restored. If you have a large meeting that makes you nervous, take time for a short guided meditation, and you'll be able to concentrate on the meeting. It can be used in several ways to calm yourself, and it can be an asset to your life.

First of all, you need to put yourself in the most comfortable position that will allow you to relax. There is no specific position; You can lie down, lie on an armed chair, or even sit on a bed with your legs crossed. You just need to be relaxed, but be careful not to take a position that will put you to sleep.

Then you have to relax. Slow and deep breathing is a good way to relax and prepare well for meditation. Another way to relax is to close your eyes and focus on the stress. Then focus on these limitations and try to drive them out of all parts of your body. Arms, legs, hair, eyes …. etc.

Once you feel relaxed, it's time to start the most important step in your meditation session. The experience outside the body. Close your eyes and imagine how your soul comes out of your body and hovers over your head. This step requires training because you may not be able to do this on the first try. When you feel your soul floating, imagine you are traveling to a place that you feel relaxed.

Guided meditation is an experience outside the body. The relaxing environment differs depending on the person who practices meditation. Some would imagine themselves on a tropical island with an exceptional landscape, while others would instead imagine themselves in a forest amidst flowers and trees. Regardless of your relaxed environment, focus on introducing yourself in the middle.

Guided meditation is about your imaginary sanctuary. Stay in your dreamy relaxation environment for as long as possible. Try to involve all of your senses. Admire the beauty of the landscape, smell the flowers, and enjoy the sounds of birds and running water. After you have finished your journey in your imaginary environment, try to concentrate on imagining that your soul will return from there until it reaches its final destination. When you return, you will feel refreshed and relieved, like coming back from a short break. During a guided meditation, you can use ambient music to help you relax.

Guided meditation is a matter of practice. Every time you do a guided meditation, try to extend your stay in your imaginary sanctuary gradually. In addition, guided meditation with practice will have a greater impact on the intense pressures of life.

PART II

There are many things that you cannot control. You cannot, for instance, determine tomorrow's weather, or derivative prices in the financial markets, or how bad the traffic will be on your way to a weekend picnic. You cannot even control the actions of others, unless through manipulation and force. Your cousin won't stop smoking unless they truly desire to do so and is open to the tools required to help them achieve this goal. In plain terms, much of what goes on in the outside world is out of your control.

On the other hand, there are things you've always had control over. Your habits, belief, emotions, and even your state of health are things you've always been able to take charge of, even if you never realized this. You've always been able to access your subconscious mind to create the peace and calm you've always desired and smoothen out those crooked areas of your life. You have the power and potential to unclutter yourself from within, so you may live a fuller, richer, healthier, more productive life. This is what hypnosis teaches us: That all of the healing begins in the subconscious. Have you ever wondered why even in hospitals with the best of care, some people don't get better even when they could've survived? It's because, on the inside, they had lost all the willpower to live. In the same, by calibrating your subconscious programming and allowing yourself to shift mentally on the inside, you will find that you unlock a new vitality and zest for life.

The conscious mind is where all your logic, willpower, and critical thinking abilities reside. It's the part of your mind to which you're most accustomed. It is where your primary thoughts intertwine and where you access your emotions, thought, and is forced to act. Your subconscious mind encompasses more nuanced elements, such as your imagination, intuition, values, beliefs, habits, and emotions. The interaction between your conscious and subconscious mind is like a one-way street, where your subconscious mind exercises strong influences on your conscious mind but hardly ever the other way round. Self-hypnosis teaches you to reverse this natural rhythm; to reach inside and rewrite the fine prints of your mind. It is only then that you may start to create remarkable changes inside of you that will shine through to the outside world.

Everyone can be hypnotized. It doesn't matter if you think your mind is forged from still, or you regard yourself as "hyper-analytical," you can reach into your own subconscious. More importantly, everyone can hypnotize themselves, and you will realize this with the techniques that will be shared soon.

Hypnosis is a state of being that's closer to daydreaming than it is to sleep, and it has an incredibly calming effect. True, some people access the hypnotic state more easily than others, but with time and practice, everyone can get it right. Hypnosis is simply meditation with a goal. Most individuals believe that your mind has to be blank for hypnosis to work, but this is not true, especially not for self-hypnosis, where the focus is concentrating on the things that screw you up from the inside and redefining them to suit you and enhance the quality of your life. Just like in meditation where you're simply relaxed physically and mentally while being very much aware of your surroundings, you can get absorbed in the calm, gentle feeling of hypnosis while also polishing your thoughts and working out the kinks of your mind.

Self-hypnosis is a powerful tool that helps you administer your thoughts and desires more effectively. Many people regard self-hypnosis as more difficult than general hypnosis because it requires a significantly higher level of practice, concentration, and discipline to truly reach into your subconscious mind, but you can do it. If you're the kind of person that's constantly plagued with negative thoughts and tendencies for depression, then self-hypnosis is a good panacea for you. It helps you clear your headspace while channeling your energies in a more wholesome and positive direction.

Self-discipline can help address so many issues; from insomnia, to stress, to an inability to concentrate. By opening yourself up to your subconscious mind, you build a bridge to your conscious mind through which you can galvanize all your creative, intuitive, and actionable thoughts in a more rewarding direction.

Self-hypnosis helps you demolish mental blocks. It may fascinate you to know that mental blocks are simply constructions in your conscious mind that reflect your perception of yourself. These mental blocks are a leading cause of your inability to concentrate, your rising stress levels, and your productivity slumps. By changing the fundamental beliefs that hold you back, you inject new life into your dreams and finding yourself feeling better at what you do and fresher all day long. The thing is, your subconscious mind is always great at executing whatever it has been programmed to accomplish, which is why you must take your time to ensure that you're asserting the right things at all times. Self-hypnosis will help you accomplish this.

As you must have already realized, your subconscious mind wields great power. This is why you must learn to master it and use it for your own enhancement. Everything you feel and think is stored in your subconscious. That natural instinct that is sometimes referred to as your 'gut' finds its root in your subconscious. It is what fuels your active mind and, ultimately, shapes your reality. Most people are confident that they believe in themselves, but they soon find that in their heart of hearts, they are filled with doubts and uncertainties. These doubts can be devastating on so many levels, including physically and psychologically, and severely limiting. The ability to rework your subconscious mind will also prove effective in helping you make these doubts fade away.

One powerful thing about self-hypnosis is how it helps you come to terms with yourself and boost progress on the journey to loving yourself. The way you feel about a particular situation is a powerful indicator of how you'll handle it in the future. Negative feelings can lead to unsavory reactions. Self-hypnosis helps ensure that emotional reactions don't overturn your life by helping you recalibrate your headspace and facilitating your ability to manage those things that trigger you while also balancing your emotions.

Self-hypnosis will help you realize that you always have a choice when it comes to how to act in a given scenario. Whether or not you agree, hard science explicitly proves that as a person, you have power over how you choose to manage every situation. Choosing anger, violent eruptions, and resentment, though you may not realize it, is still a choice that was made somewhere in the vastness of your mind. These actions could reflect badly on you or result in consequences so dire that you find yourself consumed by regret. And if there's one thing about regret, it's how corrosive it can be on your mental health. Self-hypnosis sets you on the path to self-redemption, and reclaiming the power to direct your life on your own terms and with an acute consciousness of the power that you wield.

Stages of Self Hypnosis

Modern hypnotherapists over the years have been very inventive with models of general hypnosis and self-hypnosis alike. While certain hypnosis techniques allow for a great degree of flexibility, care must still be taken to ensure that things don't spiral out of control. Of course, self-hypnosis doesn't always put you in a trance. However, you still shouldn't listen to self-hypnosis audio instruction while driving because who knows how you could react?

Also, hypnosis in all its forms is medically disapproved for use with people who have been diagnosed with schizophrenia. And while you may find yourself gaining so much from self-hypnosis sessions and feel the burning need to share your newfound treasure with friends and loved ones, it is very important that you don't apply the techniques you learn in this book on anyone else but yourself unless you become a certified hypnotherapist because the consequences of wrong use of techniques are less than desirable.

A classical self-hypnosis session is generally divided into three core parts. Usually, in modern practice, one of the stages may be skipped—especially with quick sessions—but it's important that you understand how the process works, as this is critical for you to reap the maximum benefits of the process.

Stage 1: Preparation

A self-hypnosis session shouldn't be complicated, as this will only lead to an unproductive outcome. Simplicity ensures that your goals for the session are as clear as possible and easily achievable. The following factors may be considered and rationalized in the preparation stage:

Location

It's always best for a self-hypnosis session to happen in a closed room. Your location of choice can greatly affect your convenience during the session and determine the session's tone, which is why it's absolutely important. The room should be lukewarm, have soft lighting, and should be free of disturbances. Any slight distraction, like a pet walking across the room, can totally disrupt a self-hypnosis session, especially for beginners.

Solitude

As already established, distractions can adversely impact the success of a self-hypnosis session. Make sure your doors and windows are closed, and phones and alarms are kept silent. If you're expecting an important call, then ensure that you take it before beginning the session. In fact, complete all outstanding work before beginning the session, because nothing should bog down your mind while you're trying to balance it.

Posture

Just like in meditation, your posture can play a big role in the efficacy of your self-hypnosis session. Determine where you'll sit. Your most preferred chair in the room will do just fine. There's also the issue of how to sit. You don't want to finish a self-hypnosis session with a nagging back pain, so avoid slouching and other poor sitting postures. For best results, sit straight and relaxed, with your arms and legs uncrossed.

Outfit

Loose, simple clothes are encouraged. Sweat shorts, for instance, are ideal for a self-hypnosis session. Avoid tight-fitting clothes because they might get very uncomfortable during the session, and when this happens, you'll get distracted.

Goals

Like all important self-help tools, a self-hypnosis session must be engaged with a purpose. You're not just doing it for the activity, you must be focused on the impact. Because of the methodical nature of self hypnosis, it always helps to have a definitive target. It doesn't have to be extraordinary: It may simply be a means to achieve deep relaxation for you, or an exercise to attain mental peace, or a tool to deal with emotional trauma. It could be anything.

The first stage of self-hypnosis is vital, especially the setting of goals. Through it, you become mentally ready to break bad habits, boost your brain function, overcome negativity, and much more.

Stage 2: Induction

Induction symbolizes the functional starting point of self-hypnosis. Induction is what truly opens you up to your subconscious and begins the process of self-healing. It is generally advised, then, that induction shouldn't be launched abruptly, but rather slowly and methodically. You should also consider the following at this stage:

Shut Down Your Thoughts

Thoughts here doesn't refer to the blanket of ideas and information that roam around your mind in every waking moment. It refers to stray thoughts that are completely uncorrelated with the agenda of the session. Some self-hypnosis sessions require you to shelve all thoughts, but others such as emotional hypnotherapy may require you to screen certain thoughts and reactions. Still, it would be generally unhelpful to make dinner plans even while trying to achieve self-hypnosis.

Breathing Technique

The way you breathe can significantly affect the quality of a self-hypnosis session. Good breathing techniques get you relaxed and get you in the right frame of mind. Slow, deep breathing has also been shown to possess significant health benefits.

Close Your Eyes

More than half of the distractions around you can be eliminated by simply closing your eyes. It slows the world around you down and can have a very calming effect. We connect with the world first through our eyes, so by breaking this connection, we find it easier to focus on what's going on inside.

Imagination

For self-hypnosis to work, you need to get to a place of relaxation and pure focus. Make your imagination vivid and colorful and reflective of your deepest desire. If you want to feel grounded, imagine yourself as a mountain. If you want to feel untethered and truly free, visualize yourself as a bird, taking flight in the cloudless sky. The more detailed it is, the easier it'll be for your mind to accept it.

Determine Tension Spots

Over time, tensions begin to gather in different parts of the average person's body. For a self-hypnosis session to be maximally productive, you have to eliminate this tension. Start with your toes and work your way slowly toward your head, feeling, or the tension in each body part. It's helpful to imagine the tension as a clogged dam when you find a spot. Massage the spot slowly and feel the tension dissipate. Imagine it like a stream, flowing gently away.

Statements

This is where the true magic of self-hypnosis begins to take effect. You already have a goal for the session. Select a statement that aligns with it. Make it definitive and straightforward. So, say your goal for the session is reducing stress, say things like 'I am no longer stressed' or "Stress has vanished from my life." Making the statement firm and unambiguous enables you to reprogram your subconscious and achieve the desired impact.

When you feel yourself starting to feel woozy, try saying the statement in a loop. Begin by saying it slowly, 5 times a minute, with breaks in between for deep breaths. Once you get comfortable with it, increase the rate to 10, then 20, then 30, and beyond.

The induction stage is critical because this is where you work yourself into a state of self-hypnosis. Don't be afraid to delve deep, and be wary of your thoughts.

Stage 3: Consistency

Self-hypnosis is definitely not a one-time wonder. It takes consistent practice and discipline to harness its true benefits. It requires you to seize every opportunity that you have to reiterate the statements that you selected during the induction phase, in the car, at the office, in the restroom, while taking out the trash, and everywhere else when the opportunity presents itself.

You must also realize that it is important to implement lifestyle changes where they are relevant for the accomplishment or the goal(s) for which you took up self-hypnosis. You must abstain from harmful habits and take deliberate steps to manage your anger better. Giving in to the temptations that made you consider self-hypnosis in the first place will only set you back.

You should also work on the following:

Focus

You may initially find it hard to clear out stray thoughts during a self-hypnosis session. It happens to everyone. Select the nearest object and focus on it. Observe the patterns and contours on its surface, then try to phase them out. With a few attempts, you'll find that it becomes easier to blur these patterns from the scope of your vision. This will make it easier for you to banish stray thoughts, in readiness for a self-hypnosis session.

Fix Your Trigger

Fear and doubt are two important triggers that you must dominate to make the most out of self-hypnosis. In the process of self-healing, doubt can be a serious dampener. The more you question your chances of getting better, the harder you will find it to connect with the core of your subconscious mind and put it all together.

Fear can make you undermine your capacity for growth and progress. Negative events can make you indecisive about your abilities and unsure of your potentials. By changing the way you view these events, you may find that they are helpful in that they are opportunities for you to interrogate what you could've done better. Don't shy away from the negativity of events that impacted your self-confidence. Rather, use them as a benchmark to remind yourself of how much you've grown and how much better you are now. You will find that through this, you cure yourself of emotional trauma.

Create Anchor Points

Anchor points are useful because they are an appendage for relaxation but cost nothing. Find an accessible part of your body, say your elbow, and associate it with calm and relaxation. As you do so, think of someone or something that makes you calm and relaxed. Then imagine you're with this person or doing this thing, even as you touch this anchor point. Remember, the more vivid the visualization that more you're assured that your mind will believe it. Reinforce the anchor point anytime you touch it by telling yourself in unequivocal terms that you are now calm.

It is good practice to start and end sessions with your anchor point. At the beginning of the session, close your eyes and touch the anchor point. Inhale, exhale, then slowly count backward from 10. At the end of the session, repeat the same process, opening your eyes only after you're done counting back from 10.

Relieving Stress in 60 Seconds Through Self Hypnosis

Stress is scary and damaging. It poisons moods and cuts productivity in half. When the brain produces too much of the stress hormone cortisol, it begins to operate from a place of fear. As we've already established, fear is problematic because it causes you to question your capacity for growth and really slows down your progress.

Another reason you need to work on chronic stress is how it spreads so much that it clouds other aspects of your life. A wait at the bank isn't intrinsically stressful. It's inconvenient, yes, and maybe at a point frustrating, but not stressful in its own right. Yet, many people in a similar scenario would be quick complaining about how the wait is stressing them out. This is because your brain is churning out cortisol on overdrive. The technique below promises to help detoxify you from the free radicals that clog up your happiness.

Try to read through the directions a few times and internalize the process, especially because glancing at your phone for each step could severely distract you. For now though, the most important thing is that you let your self relax.

Directions

On a scale of 0–10, sincerely determine your actual stress levels, where 0= No stress and 10= Panic attack mode. As you practice self-hypnosis more regularly, you will find yourself scoring a 0. Remember this number that you have determined.

Get yourself comfortable in a silent, closed, moderately lit room.

Select your best chair and place your feet flat on the ground. Position your hands gently in your laps.

Take 4 deep, slow breaths and exhale slowly 4 times for 8 counts. Keep your back straight but comfortable.

With your eyes totally shut, count down from 10 to 1 very slowly. After each number, say "I am delving deeper." As in: Ten, I am delving deeper, Nine, I am delving deeper...

Try Hypno-affirmations. Take another slow, deep breath, and say out loud: I am safe, I am free, I am hereby choice.

Exercise your imagination. With another slow, deep breath, imagine that you're happy for the rest of the day. Make the visual clear, colorful, and convincing. Tell yourself that nothing can stress you today.

After about a minute of imagining a happy rest of the day, open your eyes and let the wave of calm wash over you.

Stretch your arms over the top of your head and say 'Yes!'.

Determine your new stress ranking on a scale of 0–10, where 0= No stress, and congratulate yourself for the progress made.

Overcoming Pain With Self Hypnosis

Self-hypnosis can accelerate healing in unimaginable ways. It can help with expediting recovery from nausea in chemotherapy patients and the healing of bones. It can bring comfort and ease to any area of your body that's experiencing pain or discomfort. Extensive conditioning with a certified hypnotherapist can completely replace surgeries and anesthesia, but while that may be out of reach for a individual engaging self-hypnosis, you'll still be able to remedy headaches, body pains, and general aches.

Directions

Get comfortable. Wear loose clothes and find a closed, moderately lit room.

Sincerely, determine your stress ranking on a scale of 0–10, where 0 is the absolute minimum level of stress the most relaxed person can accomplish. Remember this number.

Sit in a comfortable chair and keep your spine straight and comfortable. Ensure your feet are flat on the ground, and your palms are rested on your laps.

Take 4 slow, deep inhales, and 4 corresponding exhales for a count of 8.

Close your eyes and imagine yourself as your favorite plant. Feel your roots spread from your feet and push gently below the Earth's surface, grounding you.

Imagine your favorite color as a light. Let it flow all over you, right from the depths of your roots at the center of the Earth to the tips of your fingers and the crown of your head.

You may begin to feel a tingling sensation, like a heartbeat, in your palms. Concentrate on this feeling. Direct all your attention to the feeling in your palms and get comfortable with it. As you do so, breathe for at least 20 seconds.

With your eyes still closed, count down from 10 to 1, saying, "I am delving deeper." after every number.

Silently, but preferably out loud, say the following Hypno-affirmations 10 times: I am safe, I am improving, I send my _____(name a part of your body)_____ love and calm, I feel better already.

Focus on the part(s) of your body that are experiencing pain individually. With expansive breaths, visualize all the pain draining out from that part of your body. Feel the warm, soothing energy of healing caress that spot. Feel and experience the healing sensation wash over you.

After about 2 minutes of visualizing yourself getting healed, imagine that favorite color as a wave of light once again. But this time, let it cascade down from the top of your head to the soles of your feet, and then down to your roots in the center of the Earth.

Exhale and allow yourself to feel relief. Stretch your hands above your head and say, "Yes!"

Determine your new ranking on the stress scale. Congratulate yourself for your progress with transforming your state positively.

Don't be afraid to let your love wash over you. And you can be flexible with your choice of color during the session on pain reduction. What matters the most is that you don't restrict your mind and that you trust yourself enough to reprogram your mind and heal yourself.

Is Overcoming Anxiety Possible?

Anxiety is a very strong sensation. It's a more advanced form of panic attacks, can completely destabilize you and break your focus. It's erroneous to view anxiety like some alien sensation fashioned to destroy you. Anxiety is very connected to your natural fight or flight tendencies. For instance, if you were walking down a dark alley and heard metal scraping against a wall in the distance, you could conclude that it was a knife and suddenly find yourself overcome with anxiety, adrenaline, and fear. In this scenario, it's perfectly explainable. Psychologists have found that certain stimuli are universal in the way they trigger fight or flight tendencies. In the case of a fear of getting stabbed in a dark alley, this fear makes sense.

Anxiety may be rational or irrational, and irrational anxiety does get problematic, but it isn't possible to be anxious for no reason. If, say, you had an all-important job interview tomorrow, while you may be very prepared for it, it is reasonable to expect that you may wake up sweating by 3 AM, nervous and full of anxiety. And while this is not nearly as rational a reason for anxiety as in the alleyway instance where your life was in danger, it still suffices. Most folk, however, find that they feel anxiety over minute things, such as everyday conversations, going out in public, or going to work.

Overcoming anxiety is very possible. This is because there is always an underlying reason for whatever we feel as individuals. As long as we can narrow down on the source of the anxiety, it becomes easy to eliminate it. However, the real problem for most individuals who suffer from anxiety attacks is that their anxiety comes from a very ambiguous place. They couldn't possibly place it even if they tried.

Some psychologists argue that the ultimate reason for anxiety is to trigger you to take action, especially seeing as it's connected to one of your most fundamental tendencies as an individual. In the interview instance stated earlier, the anxiety could be helpful to the extent where it pushes you to go through your notes again, crosscheck and verify that your clothes are still good to go, and put finishing touches on your presentation. By ensuring that you're at your most prepared, your chances of securing the job and attaining economic security become higher. In this case, the anxiety served in the line of a specific purpose, and, in this scenario, as you begin to realize that you're as prepared as you'll ever be, you'll find that the anxiety vanishes. Have you ever observed your anxiety fading away once you start taking action towards the goal of addressing the anxiety-causing issue?

The most problematic kind of anxiety is that which the roots are ambiguous. This is what we'll focus the bulk of our energy in this section toward eradicating. In English Language, there are over 2500 words describing a vast range of emotions, yet when most people are asked how they feel, they tend to be able to provide only about a dozen words. Even more interestingly, studies have shown that many individuals end up repeating the same dozen words week after week. For this category of people, the mind and body are two separate worlds that don't intersect. As a result of this, they tend to label their emotions rather than truly experience them.

If self-hypnosis teaches anything at all, it's that your strongest internal powers are only unlocked when you become attuned with your mind. All emotions find their roots in the subconscious mind, and the stronger your mind-body connection, the easier you'll find the process of parsing your emotions. Most emotions start off with similar fundamental sensations and maintain this similarity all the way through in many instances. This is why some people find the ambiguous sensation of stage fright terrifying, while others find it exciting and exhilarating. Your reaction to these sensations, hence, is a product if your self-perception.

Thus you will find that positive emotional labeling has a potent therapeutic effect. Overcoming anxiety becomes easily attainable once you learn to truly experience your emotions before attempting to label them and then describe them in a positive light. For instance, based solely on your perspective, a stimulus that was meant to trigger euphoria, excitement, pride in yourself tends to always be summarized as "happiness." In the same vein, a stimulus that was meant to inspire nervousness, excitement, and worry simply becomes "anxiety." As a result, a situation could present a stimulus that is supposed to excite you, but you end up getting anxious because you misinterpreted it.

To see how easily you can set yourself on the path to overcoming anxiety, let's engage this quick exercise. Imagine yourself as a decorator who has been trained to understand the nuances of color. Now, think of your emotions as colors. You may find that primary colors pop up in your mind. That's fine. Concentrate on each color, and then multiply it with at least 4 substitutes. Transform the blues into aquamarine, cyan, teal, and iris. Decompose the reds into pink, ruby, magenta, and sangria.

Now, let us transmit the breakthrough above toward dealing with your emotions. Now, take a moment to recall a vivid memory where you felt what you believed was anxiety. Look for a memory that you can recall in detail, preferably one where the anxiety only seemed to worsen with time. Now, grab a pen and paper. In your own words, describe how you felt at the time. Now, write out 10 words that succinctly and accurately describe your state of mind in that precise moment: you could've said you felt gloomy, even though you were only slightly saddened, or you could've said you were nervous, even if you were actually excited. Use a dictionary or thesaurus to find the words that best describe your emotions at the time, if you need to.

Scrutinize your list of 10 words. Of the ten, which emotions give you the most positive outlook of the situation as compared to the anxiety you thought you were feeling? Write them out separately. As was established previously, most emotions start out with the same sensations and maintain a consistent similarity all through. So, imagine how differently that situation would've turned out if you had labeled your emotions at the time through these positive lenses instead. Does the situation suddenly feel different in your head?

If you were to apply this technique to events that happen in your life daily, you'd find that it suddenly becomes easier to cancel out negative emotions. Repeat this exercise over and over, focusing on a different emotion each time. You'll realize in no time that anxiety will no longer surface, because you have now cultivated the ability to replace it with more desirable emotions.

How Do You Overcome Anxiety?

Your emotions speak to you all the time. There's a robust internal communication system inside of you that is highly developed, but you can only bring out its true potential when you learn the controls of it. In the last exercise, you learned how to cancel out negative emotions of anxiety in memory (and even in concurrent events) by labeling them more positively or replacing them with brighter emotions. In this section, you'll learn even more advanced techniques. Primarily, you'll be exposed to the rudiments of listening to your emotions and how this can help you overcome anxiety. After this, you'll learn how to manipulate the technique of visualization for your emotional advantage. Finally, you'll learn how to use the technique of dissociation with a practical example.

Let's begin with listening to your emotions. At this point, you must have realized the deep relevance of maintaining a strong connection with all facets of your mind, especially your subconscious mind. Your subconscious mind communicates with your body, which is why it makes sense that we're first hit by our feelings before thoughts. It generally works in this way: (1) Your subconscious mind perceives a stimulus and generates some response, which is sometimes referred to as a stress response (2) Your conscious mind scans the environment and tries to attach these stimuli to external objects or concepts, with these attachments manifesting as feelings (3) Having attached the stimulus to your external environment, you are now poised to take action.

If you were camping in the woods and you came across a snake, your fight or flight instincts would kick in instantly. Your heart rate would skyrocket, and your senses would heighten. Adrenaline would fill you from the inside in a mad rush. In this scenario, you're feeling strong emotions and, more importantly, you know why you're feeling them. Whatever decision you decide to take here—whether to run or stay and confront the snake—is entirely at your discretion and instinct. As you can see, there are multiple possibilities to choose from in terms of your emotions. You could let fear take over, or you could welcome boldness and deep resolve. In the same way, you become more conscious of the stimuli your subconscious mind processes, you will find that you will always have choices rather than anxiety to pick from in every scenario.

Most times, when we feel discomfort, stress, or anxiety, they're actually signals that our subconscious is trying to alert us to a problem. It may be sending you this message because you have left important tasks unresolved, or because you have paused integral plans in your life and ignored them completely. It could be alerting you because your struggles are creating internal friction and destabilizing the alignment of your life. Your subconscious always tries to get across to you, and it's usually for very significant matters.

Have you ever considered that anxiety could simply be your mind's way of motivating you to address an issue or fix a loose end from the past that has been dangling ever since? By learning to listen to your emotions, you can better tell these messages apart and eliminate all ambiguity as regards their roots. We have already examined the tool of elimination. Now, let us consider another tool for overcoming anxiety: acknowledging and labeling emotions.

The process involves asking several questions. The next time you feel anxiety, ask yourself these questions: Why am I feeling anxious? Why do I feel this anxiety now? What is my subconscious trying to tell me?

Listen to your mind as you ask these questions. Really listen for the answer. Write in a journal as many causes as you can rationally come up with, in the context of the situation. Then take time to cross them out in order of improbability, until you arrive at one or two potential causes. What this process does is eliminate all ambiguity, as you now know the exact cause(s) of your anxiety. This newfound clarity enables you to easily tackle the sources of your anxiety quickly and overcome them without any damage to your psychological health.

Alternately if you do not have the time or aren't in the mental state to tackle your anxiety at that moment, this technique helps you to schedule a time for dealing with it in the future while at the same time breaking the hold of stress and anxiety, seeing as your subconscious will stop alerting you because you've already received the message. You want to eliminate any anchors of anxiety before you destroy it.

The second technique you may employ is visualization. Before we delve into the nitty-gritties of this technique, it is essential that we understand the power of imagery. You must have, at least at one point in your life, woken up from a dream with your heart racing. What does this tell you? It reveals that your mind cannot exactly differentiate between what occurs in the outside world and what occurs only in your mind. The point is: images are so powerful that they can convince your mind into believing things that aren't real. This attribute can be a disadvantage or an advantage, depending on how you look at it.

Sometimes an upcoming event can be so insignificant or mellow in its consequences that you can mentally brush it aside, while at other times, the event is so important that it takes up all the space your mind has to give. This is why a Saturday afternoon picnic may not bother you very much if only your family members are in attendance, but can quickly become a source of serious anxiety if, say, your boss or a client decided to join you.

When important events are coming up, the doors fling wide open for anxiety to come in. If you were to give a keynote speech at an international conference, you would definitely be under intense pressure to put your very best foot forward. This scenario provides fertile soil for anxiety to thrive. Your mind may begin to traumatize you with images of things going horribly wrong, of you forgetting your speech, or making a blunder in front of the audience, or spilling coffee on the laptop containing your slides and then having to make an extemporaneous presentation. A thousand and one thoughts may plague your mind. This is a perfect opportunity to engage the time-tested technique of visualization.

In the actual sense, all of us use visualizations, whether consciously or unconsciously. The only difference is that the average person allows the images they create to run wild and morph into negative emotions, while others who learn how to manipulate the images their minds create can control them and strengthen their minds through these images. By engaging the exercise below, you will be in a better position to take charge of the visuals in your mind and eliminate all anxiety.

To begin with, find a quiet place with mild lighting. Lie down and close your eyes. Make sure you're comfortable. Then breathe. Let your inhalations be slow, deep, and wholesome. Now, imagine the event that is causing you anxiety—let's say it's an idea pitching meeting you're having with potential investors in your company—and focus on it. Imagine it going really well. Imagine the awe on the faces of the investors as you wow them with your ideas. Imagine the charisma and finesse with which you deliver all your lines. Imagine your jokes landing perfectly. Play this image over and over in your mind, rewinding, and making each new iteration better than the last. Imagine walking out of the meeting with a look for pride and accomplishment on your face.

Think about it: After engaging this exercise, how do you think you would feel about this hypothetical pitch meeting? You would feel amazing, of course. Even more, you would have a greater chance of succeeding at it, according to several studies. You must never underestimate the power of mental images. They can play a powerful role in shaping your reality. Remember, you can make your mind believe anything. Use this power to your advantage.

Finally, let us consider the technique of mental dissociation. Dissociation is a tremendously powerful exercise that has evolved over the last few decades. It is a highly effective technique that helps catalyze mental shifts and reprogram the subconscious mind.

Dissociation involves a copious amount of visualization, but it is a lot more powerful because it helps you view yourself as others do. You become like an external observer of your own self, giving you a level of fresh insight that was previously inaccessible. You start to see your actions like recorded events and piece them together better.

For this technique to work, you'll have to zone in on a situation that causes you a lot of anxiety. Before you begin the dissociation process, all you need is a rough sketch of the situation in your mind. Don't conjure the full details yet. We will call this situation "the event."

Now, sit up tall and straight. Breathe slowly and powerfully until you feel your confidence and strength increase. To facilitate this, cast your mind back to moments when you felt strong and capable. Now, walk through the following steps:

Imagine a cinema. Imagine yourself sitting in the back row and facing the large screen. Don't forget to view this in dissociation (that is like it's all happening outside you). Imagine yourself looking at the screen. On the screen, imagine that the main actor is another dissociation of yourself. Somewhere else in the scene, imagine another relaxed version of you.

Imagine the event as a door at an edge of the screen. Imagine your main-actor self beginning to walk toward the event. Imagine that the frame pauses 20 seconds before you get to the door

Now, imagine that your character in the back row has a laptop. On that laptop, imagine a second screen in which the movie frame is also paused at the same point. With one tap of a button, the movie will continue.

Think of yourself as a movie director, determine what the character does and when and how they do it. The movie's ending is solely at your discretion. Be calm, collected, confident, and in control. Allow yourself to deal with the event that caused you trouble in the past. Make it fun and exciting. Create the best happy ending that you can imagine.

Leave your body and go with the new version of the movie to the back room. Connect the laptop to the projector.

Play the new version of the movie on the big screen and watch it until the end. Allow yourself to feel satisfaction at the fact that things are much better now.

Return to the back row and enter your body on the seat. Ensure that you like what you see with each rewatch until you're fully convinced that you have the best ending you can think of.

By getting back into your body, you switched from dissociation to association. Check your progress by reloading your memories of the anxiety episode and check how you feel about it now. You should definitely feel a lot better than you used to. With more practice, you will feel better and better, and anxiety will become less terrifying.

You may find that certain situations are so grave that you may need to attempt dissociation severally to achieve lasting results, and that's fine. The stronger the internal association you have with the memory, the more times you will have to apply dissociation to weaken the links.

How You Can Overcome Anxiety Naturally

In dealing with anxiety, most individuals have been made to believe that they can only be cured through medication. This is not only totally false, but it exposes them to the vulnerability of addiction, side effects, and chemical-induced reactions. Herbal remedies such as the poplar Kava were discovered with the hope that they would be better synthetic drugs in this regard. However, side effects such as liver damage have been associated with these herbal remedies, making them just as scary.

The good news is, there are very natural, non-drug ways to overcome anxiety. Some major natural methods are described below:

Sleep Habits

The terrible thing about anxiety is not just that it makes it harder for you to sleep; it's also that sleep deprivation fuels anxiety, sticking sufferers in an unending loop of health crises. By devoting yourself to sleeping the recommended 8 hours daily, you give your immune system the needed boost for your body to function optimally, while also equipping yourself with the strength to manage the anxiety that only a proper rest can provide.

If anxiety is making sleep inaccessible for you, you can facilitate sleep by; avoiding phone and computer screens for hours before your bedtime, ensuring that your bed is comfortable, and keeping your room's temperature well regulated.

Keep Tense Muscles in Check

Tension is fodder for anxiety. To eliminate the tension in your body, you may consider progressive muscle relaxation. You can accomplish this by choosing any muscle group of your choice, tighten it for a few seconds, and then letting it go. Do this taking each muscle group in turn.

Identify Triggers

Look for patterns in your anxiety. Are there places or events that always cause you to worry or feel anxious? Note them down and, having identified them, overcome them through self-hypnosis or mindfulness meditation techniques.

Exercise

Exercising boosts your sense of wellbeing, which in turn can help minimize your feelings of anxiety. Don't bombard yourself at the beginning. Begin with 15-minute sessions daily and then work your way up from there.

Avoid Caffeine and Alcohol

Anything with caffeine really should be avoided, from Soda to Tea, to Chocolate, to Diet Pills. Caffeinated substances raise your spirits and can be a severe trigger for anxiety. On the other hand, alcohol is a 'downer' which can also exacerbate anxiety issues.

How To Reduce Anxiety Quickly

Anxiety isn't a feeling to give one advanced notice. While you can avoid triggers and employ techniques such as self-hypnosis and visualization to overcome it, you should arm yourself with quick methods for ending unexpected anxiety episodes or panic attacks. At the same time, you work on yourself to get better.

When anxiety hits, it generally helps to find a distraction such as music. Distractions help you take your mind off the anxiousness and gather yourself together. Exercises such as jogging, running, and dancing can be instrumental in equipping you to manage anxiety better and quicker. If you're new to exercising and aren't sure that you'll be able to commit to it, you can find an exercise buddy who will motivate you to meet all your exercise goals.

Eat proper, well-balanced meals, and always have high energy snacks on hand. Managing anxiety requires both physical and mental energy, so starving yourself won't cut it. Try quick meditation techniques such as walking meditation. Also, consider getting a massage or a hot bath. These can be quite therapeutic in helping you manage anxiety. Humor has also been known to nullify the worst effects of anxiety. So, the next time to have that panic attack, try to see if you can remember something that transforms your hyperventilation into laughter.

What is Mindfulness?

Imagine for a moment that you're looking at a painting of a majestic mountain with a thick, white cloud right behind it. Mindfulness involves you seeing both the mountain and the clouds with an equal amount of attention, none surpassing the other. By applying the principle of mindfulness to your life, you're exposed to the full range of your intrinsic abilities, all laid out bare with zero noise. It shifts you from assumptive reality to one with clarity, where you can better assess yourself and track your growth.

Mindfulness entails shifting from an 'either/or' perspective to an 'and' perspective. As you make this shift, you'll find that you simultaneously outgrow all the pains—both physical and emotional—that limit you and cause you suffering. Rather than try to "get over it" or "buck up," which leaves you feeling minimized and sometimes holding a grudge, you learn true acceptance and gain access to the peace that comes along with it.

Acceptance in the context of mindfulness entails an understanding that unpleasant and unexpected things will happen, but that when they do, you still have to treat yourself with honor and kindness. It employs the principle of dissociation to the extent that it teaches you in those situations to regard yourself like you would a friend suffering. This ability to empathize with your own self makes you somewhat a best friend to yourself and has very therapeutic effects on your ability to overcome all forms of pain.

Mindfulness doubles as both a state of mind and a form of meditation. It puts you in the middle ground, ensuring that you don't deny your pain in the quest to blot out your suffering. It helps you assess all those emotions that poison your attitude to life and weaken your spirit. It further helps you to overcome physical pain and emerge stronger after each moment of peace.

Start from where you are now, even if you've never done meditation before. Pay attention to the fact that you're trying to forge a connection with your mind and remain aware of this goal. You may experience uncomfortable emotions or feel like you aren't making progress at the beginning, but trust that you are. Actively cancel out negativity and always be on the lookout to make the most of every mindfulness session.

Formal and Informal Mindfulness Practice

Meditation is the primary route through which mindfulness is practiced. It's best to have a comfortable cushion or stack of blankets to work with.

Mindfulness practice becomes formal when you dedicate a set amount of time daily toward its practice. It's like exercising; it keeps you fit and ready at all times, so you aren't moved when tricky situations arise. Because you have readied yourself through formal practice, you are equipped to take on any challenges, and your mind and body find it easier to return to equilibrium.

Walking meditation is another type of formal mindfulness practice. It involves taking long walks and taking in nature's sweetest spots, while also applying awareness and acceptance techniques through strategic meditation. Walking meditation is especially powerful because it simultaneously heals the mind and body.

Informal mindfulness practice, also called spontaneous awareness, is a means of extending the lessons from your formal mindfulness practice to the real world. It could range from random acts of kindness to strangers, to a heightened awareness of the impulses and sensations in your body as you wait in line at the coffee shop.

Getting Ready for Mindfulness Practice

One myth you must crush from the get-go is the idea that meditation must be perfect. This idea is far from the truth. It's termed mindfulness 'practice' because it may not always go a certain way, and that's fine. So, rather than waste time trying to make your sessions perfect, focus more on bringing out the most from every session by letting your internal healing energy invigorate you.

Below are some fundamental tasks that you may want to accomplish to facilitate the effectiveness of your mindfulness meditations when you begin with the techniques in the 'Guided Meditation' section.

Allocate Your Space

If possible, designate a space for your mindfulness practice. A closed, quiet, dimly lit room free from all distractions is always the way to go. Determining your designated practice space can be a motivation in itself because it ensures that you are constantly reminded of your new regimen and meet up with all your practice goals.

Gather The Necessary Materials

Put together all the props and tools that you need for a successful session and store them in the designated practice space. Writing materials, a straight-backed chair, blankets, or a soft cushion, pen and paper, and other tools you may find necessary should all be put together before you begin.

Silence Phones and Other Potentially Noisy Electronics

Even if you've never done so during waking hours, turn off your phone. If you have to keep time with it, then set it to airplane mode. In this case, do not glance at it any more than is necessary.

Determine Practice Time and Length

Mindfulness practice is known to boost the immune system and purify emotions, so you may want to designate adequate time to it. Your sessions should occur at a particular time daily and should span at least 25 minutes.

Prepare Comfortable Clothes

As much as it is possible, wear loose, comfortable clothing. Meditation gurus also generally advise that people dress in layers during mindfulness practice. Ensure that you don't wear anything that constricts you physically.

Establish Your Posture

Sit with your back straight and let your hands rest naturally on your thighs, palms face down. Ensure that your spine is as elongated as possible by tilting your back, but be careful not to arch your back forward or backward. Relax your jaw, but let the space between your upper and lower teeth be little. Your lips should be parted slightly, while your tongue should simply rest against the upper front row of your teeth. Your legs should be apart, uncrossed, and flat on the floor, with your knees pointed at right angles. If you tend to hunch forward, raise the heart center of your chest slightly to prevent this. Finally, tuck in your chin slightly so that your head feels level.

If you decide to go the way of the traditional masters by sitting cross-legged on the floor, do so over a zafu. If you cannot find one, then you may substitute it with a stack of soft blankets. Rather than restricting yourself to a rigid seat, picture yourself sitting with relaxed dignity. Position your body as in the 'sitting in a chair' instance in the last paragraph, the only difference should be in the posture of your legs. You may cross your legs in front of you or just above your ankles. You may alternately shift one leg in front of the other so that they remain uncrossed if crossing them will be inconvenient for you. Your hips should be above your knees at all times, and your knees should be on the floor.

It is also important that you note that there is no such thing as a bad meditation. As you're very likely new to this, you may find it to be a bit of a learning curve, especially for the first 8 sessions. However, as you immerse yourself further in mindfulness practice, you'll find that you only get better at it. Also, you may have already picked this up, but it's still important to reiterate that meditation and mindfulness practice doesn't necessarily equate to eradicating all your thoughts. You must realize that there are sessions where you will have to meditate on certain thoughts so you can connect with your subconscious mind.

Mindfulness practice helps you manage emotional fallouts through focused practice. Learn to trust the process and never limit any sensations you feel during guided meditation. You may also find yourself getting sleepy during mindfulness practice. This is bound to happen mostly when you're suffering from insomnia and sleep deprivation. Meditation relaxes you, so you could become so calmed that the tiredness in your body starts to reflect. When this happens, by all means, sleep. It's exactly what you need.

Finally, you must be cautious with your use of meditation in situations of trauma. Mindfulness practice does teach body awareness and emotional awareness, both of which are integral to increasing our innate capacity to handle trauma. However, trauma also brings along with it strong, intrusive images and sometimes auditory hallucinations. In this case, it is risky to attempt healing yourself alone. You should consider working with a trauma-sensitive mindfulness instructor or a therapist, even as you boost your recovery through meditation.

Guided Meditation

Guided meditation helps you achieve mindfulness and internal awareness through structured meditation guidelines. Below are a number of meditation exercises to get you started:

Breathing Exercises

These should take no longer than 10 minutes.

Keep your mouth completely closed but very relaxed. Inhale and exhale through your mouth in a rapid sequence, ensuring that your breathing is equal all through, and the breaths are short. This exercise is rather loud, but you'll get accustomed to it with time.

Work toward a breathing cycle of 3 sharp inhalations and exhalations per second. This will lead to rhythmic movements in your diaphragm. If you find that you're beginning to get fatigued, pause, resume regular breathing for one minute, and then return to the breathing cycle.

Breath Counting

This exercise should last for 10–15 minutes.

Sit in a comfortable position with your back straight.

Inhale slowly and deeply and begin shutting your eyes slowly.

Exhale powerfully but slowly. You want to achieve a consistent rhythm.

Do not restrain your thoughts. Let incoming thoughts flow in, but let them go quickly. Return to your breathing, ensuring that the thoughts don't distract you to the point of breaking your rhythm.

Imagine a wave of light flowing from your head to your feet and back. Watch it pulsate as you breathe.

Be mindful of the sensations that occur in all areas of your body that the light passes through.

Don't change these sensations. Aim instead to recognize them and, the moment you do, let them go. The goal is simply to heighten your awareness of these sensations.

Count to 'five' as you exhale. Be careful to breathe out very slowly. Do this over and over.

Do not count higher than five. Once you go beyond it, note that you have been distracted.

Acceptance and Observation Exercises

This helps you concentrate on accepting your pain and finding mental peace, calm, and relief from pain.

Assume a comfortable position with your back straightened and well supported. You can begin this session seated on a straight-backed chair or lying face-up on your back.

Imagine yourself as a calm, distant observer. Pay attention to how you're feeling at the moment. Don't attempt to change it; simply observe and acknowledge.

Pain management begins with observation. Scan your body and identify where the pain and tension resides. Where is all the pain located? What parts of your body are calm and at ease?

Notice all sensations, subtle and strong, in all areas that you scan.

Take a deep inhaling breath and release it in a long exhale. Keep breathing slowly and calmly. In... Out... In again.

Pay close attention to all the sensations your body is feeling. The cold air flowing in through your nostrils. The smoothness of the floor beneath your feet. Paying attention to all these sensations could easily distract you. Be aware of this and restore your attention the moment you do so. Anchor your focus to your breath, so it always brings you back.

Keep observing everything. Your breaths, as they switch from shallow to deep. Observe where your body is tight and free. Feel the pain stored up across your body. Imagine them as knots and unravel them. Watch the pains flow slowly away. Don't judge them, just accept them and let go.

Internal Healing

You may be seated on the floor or in a chair. Whichever you choose, be sure to relax in a comfortable position.

Allow your thoughts to pass through with calmness and acceptance. Focus on your breath. Take in slow, deliberate streams of air. Exhale slowly and calmly. Do this 5 more times, focusing on your breath all the way.

Begin observing your present thoughts. Pay special attention to the thoughts of pain. You have a strong urge to change these thoughts, don't you? Fight the temptation. Simply understand these thoughts, don't try to change them.

Begin labeling your thoughts. As you do, distance yourself from these thoughts. Aim for an understanding that the thoughts are merely transient. They will not always be here, and they do not define who you truly are.

Inhale and exhale as calmly as you can. Don't break the cycle. Now that you've labeled your thoughts, focus your attention on your breathing.

Focus on the discomfort points in your body. Imagine an alternate sensation. It could be anything, anything other than the sensation of pain. If you feel a tingle in your arms or legs, embrace it. This gives you control over your physical sensations.

Immerse yourself fully in this sensation. Feel it replacing your fears and overriding your feelings of pain. Take it one step at a time and, slowly, watch your pain fade away.

Allow yourself to absorb the energy of passively embracing your feelings and thoughts. Distance yourself from them. Feel the healthy sensation that this distance brings. Let yourself bask in this sensation.

At this juncture, be aware of all the things your senses perceive. Notice each sound that flows into your ear. Observe how your clothes sit on your body. Focus on all the thoughts that this observation brings. Label them.

Mentally scan your body from the top of your head to the sole of your feet. Peacefully move along with your body. Don't judge or excessively moderate the sensations you feel at this point. Simply accept them. When you reach your feet, bring attention back to your breath for a final time. Inhale slowly, then exhale.

Open your eyes.

Chapter Two:
Stories Of The Siberia

NORTHERN LIGHTS

There is something absolutely satisfying about visiting an old place with friends. The pleasure of rediscovering someplace absolutely forgotten, experiencing a sight you once beheld as magical but have now dismissed. It is like finding that old sweater you wore a lot as a child or blowing the dust off a childhood diary and burrowing into the comfort of old thoughts. Except this time, you visit with new eyes and places once forgotten take on new light. There is less this time to see and more to experience with the senses of others, a shared companionship.

And so it is that when your plane touches down in the evening, all of your senses immediately come alive, tingling in anticipation of all the wonders to be beheld and seen. You have just arrived in Siberia, a region in Russia, spanning Eurasia and North Asia and home to long, harsh winters and home right now, of course, to you and your company of traveling friends.

It is a quiet winter, and the air is crisp, still, almost expectant. You are standing on the shores of Russia's heartland, your feet protected from the cold with layers of warm, wool clothing, and thick snug boots. This forgotten northern outpost has lost prominence when easier routes across Siberia opened up. And it is why you have chosen here in Nayan-Mar as the spot from which you and your friends will observe the Aurora Borealis – a little more silence, a little more daring. The treasure of knowing you now walk paths that many have forgotten to tread. With the legends and myths that follow your footsteps, you feel as though all of the universe has ushered you to this moment. You cannot help but want to whistle, a sound you know the mountain's echoes will carry along and bring back to you, a returned gift from nature. But you stop yourself – the majesty of this night begs a reverence, a refusal to stain such with spontaneity. It feels as though if you moved too fast, Nature might startle and move away. And so you swallow your whistle, but your mind carries the tune as far as your head can think it. Ooh-ooh-lah-lah-ooh. The perfect rhythm to a perfect night.

Your hands run along your arms, up and down, up and down as though to warm away from the cold. But you are not cold tonight. Rather, your hands enclave your arms in a warm, loving hug. You wish as you do that, you could trap all of these memories in yourself as your warm wool has trapped all of the heat. It seems as you warm yourself with a hug that you would offer the universe one if you could.

Your eyes should be taking in the beautiful landscape and watching the majestic terrain, but your gaze is fixed firmly above on the inky expanse of a starry midnight sky. Above you, the night skies have transformed the world about you into a fairy-tale. The atmosphere is electric and has taken a hopeful tinge upon them. Anything is possible tonight.

In this wilderness of darkened hue, you sit with your friends and wait. Pause. The sound of your breaths fills up the space between you, but you cannot notice. You are transfixed, your gaze set on the mystic sky above. And then...a flicker. Are you holding your breath now? Tiny disturbances in the earth's cover have held you spellbound.

Is that...? – a friend makes to say.

But your finger moves to his lips to shush him before he can get the word out. You nod. Yes. That is. You stare at the awe in their eyes, and you see mirrored there, the marvel on your own. The northern lights in her vivid electromagnetic charm have held you all, and your eyes follow the path of the luminous green light as it shuffles across the sky. Greens and blues and pinks dance a star's song into being while the sky stretches and wakes up and prepares to host this fit of brilliance. You blink, and the night skies seem to wink back at you. Your hearts sigh, and in awe of the wonder you have just beheld, it seems that the universe sighs as well.

NOMADIC PASTORALS

Winding down from a long day, this will help you, Relaxation will find you as you drift further and further down into a night of restorative and blissful night sleep. Find a cozy, safe place where you may lay down, where you can drift off without distractions and interactions. The most important thing to note right now is how much you deserve this time of rest. You may let go of lingering thoughts and allow yourself to feel the pride that comes with making it through another day. Let go of any concerns you may have about tomorrow, the day after that, or the future.

Imagine that you have squirreled these concerns and worries away into a box and set them on a bedside table where they will await you tomorrow when you are ready and better equipped with an hour of rest to tackle these challenges. This story will take you to the night of a young girl nomad as she lies awake at night, thinking through the journeys she has made.

"Go to Sleep," they said to Arya. But Arya only wanted to stare at the sky through the hole in her tent. Through the hole, she could hear the wind whipping through the land, teasing all who hear and daring any who could catch him. Ooooooooh. Ooooooooh. Again, and again, the wind whipped through the land. Oooooooooooooooooooh. Oooooooooooooooooh. It seemed like it went on for longer this time, as though forcing any who tried to catch him to first catch their own breath.

Beyond the frame of the hearty laughter of the wind, its soft cackles, and its howling, fierce ragings, young Arya tried again to stare at the skies. She had become familiar with the wind and the skies in her many travels. Several rooms zipping through strange lands have taught her to look out for the details that matter. Arya, aged only eleven, had decided that those were the two that did the wind and the skies. No more is needed to tell a story of a land and its people than the winds and the skies, Arya's trusty companions. And tonight, as she listens to the winds tell its secrets of the places he's seen and the people he's met, she needs the skies to nod at the tales. Is that true, she would ask silently? Her ears and eyes darting between both wind and skies. Is that true what the wind says, Sky? Is there truly a man in this land with a farm large as this traveling band. What? – can his entire servanthood dwarf even our herd of cattle? Is that true, Sky? Is that true what the wind says? And in its usual calming, soothing town, the wind whispers back, Oooooooh, yes.

Tonight, young Arya cannot sleep again and so she asks her dear friends, the wind for a story. There's a strangely comforting smell of sheep poop and fur left behind by the last herd that passed through. This, she can tell. She had time to look around before Papa set up the tent and banished her to bed. There's a small grove of oaks, and it's quiet except the small wet wind you can hear pass you by in the cool autumn night. It's a large vast field and her family, pastoral nomads have brought their herd through this vast agricultural site. Sometimes, at night, she can hear a cow move, the indistinct slug of his body as it takes a drink of his water, and she can imagine the lazy blink of its eyes. She pulls all of these from memory.

Once, aged nine, she had snuck away from her parents to watch nature in its full, untapped glory, and she had been awed. She had found a forest with aged white pines by a hamlet off the path her parents had taken. This special place held her in awe for a while, and the silence of the place made it more enchanting. Away from the marching hooves of her father's cows, this lovely place was a soft respite from the sometimes-marching nomadic life.

A dew forms on the emerald-green form of a lush leaf, and she finds that those of the community have adorned trees with miniature sculptures and pieces of art. She feels the damp earth beneath her sandals and hears a twig occasionally crunch or twitch beneath her feet. She is embraced by the warmth she feels here. Rays of light create prism with the dew that covers the forest floor. The night is golden and warm, like kindness filling the inner forest with a sort of welcoming halo. She studies the earth-brown and leaf-green of her surroundings and, like children often do, lets out a burst of tinkling laughter. She is amazed, pleased to find in the oft-monotony of nature, a sliver of creation that amazes and draws her in.

Are you still with this story? Allow all of your joints to sink into the head. Allow your limbs, hands, and necks to simply feel this relaxation together. Remember to take deep breaths as you do this. Take in air and hold it in, allowing It to fill your lungs. Then, just sigh it out, audibly, if you want. Inhale again for Three, two, one, and then let all this air out. You can repeat this again and again as you desire.

As she stared, Arya wondered what it would be to feel like a century-old tree, rooted and grounded in the earth. And suddenly, she began to feel like she was in the exact right place at the time. The wind whispered, and the skies above her echoed her. And from that day, the world was Arya's friend.

REINDEERS

Allow yourself to fall asleep tonight to the sounds from this beautiful sleep story. Immerse yourself here and choose the experiences you connect to and how far you are willing to go before you settle into dreamland. This may be time for intricate self-care. Go ahead- light that jasmine-scented candle and let the warm glow that fills your room fill your heart also. Inhale. Exhale. Allow yourself time for introspection too – flip through the pages of your mind, of your heart, and accept the memories you find there. Wonder at each one, stare in curiosity, and let your heart take you with these memories where your head would only grudgingly go.

This time is especially for you – for self-care and happy fun. It is the time before you are welcomed into dreaming, restorative sleep, it is your right to take the time for deep rest. You are deserving of it. You may now appreciate the bed beneath you, the softness of your wool blanket, and that humidness to the air as though all of Nature and the angels have held their breath in awe at first and then released a collective exhale. Revel in the fact that you have made it through another day.

As you listen, think about my voice as that of a dear and trusted friend, one who may guide you to a comfortable place to get cozy without distraction and interactions from the outside world. Here, you may just let go and breathe, allow yourself to be authentic. Just real, true to who you are, loving and accepting every facet and tenet of yourself. You have made it through your day and soared through the waves of constant change and transition to show victory. If there are things you wish to change, you know that you can. Nothing lasts forever, and you are capable of changing your story still. You are in charge.

Let go now and allow yourself to be transported to the charming community where my story is set. At any point in this story, you may choose to let go of my voice and find your own story. This story is groomed by your own desires and needs. Take a deep breath. Inhale. Exhale. Let go of your breath, audibly, if you care to. Again, do that. take a deep breath in and allow yourself to savor the feel of the breath in your lungs. Then slowly, slowly, let the air out. Through your nostrils and your mouth, if you want. There? Do you feel yourself becoming grounded and becoming lighter, letting go of your today's worries? Watch yourself gather up the worries and fears like little bits of shredded, white paper and blow them into the air. Watch them in your mind's eye as they fall to the ground like little bits of nothing. Sigh it out and feel the back of your heavy eyelids that press upon your eyes, shutting out the pressures of the outside world.

Watch this enchanting scene unfold before you as though a blackout curtain has been pulled down before you. You are now in the magical theatre where you will watch this story play out. But first, take a deep breath again. You must ground yourself at this moment. Exhale. Let it all out. Can you smell it now? The warmth of ageless pines in a large clearing. Above you, soft snowflakes drop in an endearing fall, as though afraid to bother the world about you. As you stare, the white expanse of land before you seem to stretch for as far as your eyes can see and your head can dare comprehend.

There Is a stillness to the air. No man moves, not even you, and you are entranced by this majestic sight before you. Your feet are snugly wrapped in woolen socks and outlined by your best comfortable boots. You tuck your hands into the knit of your oversized sweater and run your fingers along it. It is comfortable out here – you do not want to leave. Your hands drop to pick up the thermos you have packed to enjoy this view. Your hands clutch around it, and you open it to drink your favorite warm beverage that is much appreciated on this morning. The sun rises higher, and you can feel the warm sliver on your face.

You are at rest, as though the boulder that had been tied to your neck has now been removed. You feel as if you are even floating and drifting, the crisp air around you enveloping you. You cover up all the thermos and savor the memory of that warm drink, its honeylike essence moving down your throat in a liquid embrace. Your eyes close at that. it has been a beautiful morning. You set the thermos back into your bag, settling it against your extra blanket, and then begin to walk. This morning is purely for yourself, so no music accompanies you. Only the soft falls of your footsteps are present in your contemplation.

The road you have chosen this morning is one you have taken before, and so you walk purely by memory. It has been a while since you first walked this path, and your memories threaten to fail you. But you are not panicked – you know that even if you do not find the way, it would be okay. The morning has been a blessing, a gift to you already.

You take a right leading you towards a narrower clearing. You know you have taken the right turn because you can hear the distant moving sounds of a nearby creek. Whooosh – the sound seems to go right by your ears, and you are comforted by the sound of nature. Soon, you are greeted by the iconic statue of a reindeer, and this heralds your entrance into the park. You sigh and stare in wonder. Whose idea was it, you think, to put this statue up? But it is a question built of awe. You are glad – you would like to thank this person, such a beautiful idea. Now, the statue seems to welcome you into the haven.

You caress the straps of your backpack, which has been lightly packed for this long stroll into the woods. You hoist and re-hoist the shoulder straps, and the symphony of crickets and frogs around you lend a theme song to your otherwise unremarkable entrance. A miniature sculpture of another reindeer graces the gate as you push it open gently. The creaking sound it makes is music to your ears. You begin the walk up the park, and occasional crunch marks your steps as it hits a crackling leaf.

Something about this place is an essence that draws you. You first found this place years ago when you were at a time in your life such as this, and despite your many promises, only now have you found your way back to the place your heart calls sanctuary. The Reindeer Park. Your heart leaps in expectation as you gaze upon nature's canvas of cool browns and exciting greens. You can see what the owners have done to make the place even more comfortable. Tiny bells have been hoisted on trees, and as the wind whispers through the land, the bells let out a soft tinkle. And your whole body vibrates with the pleasure of this sound – it is almost as if the sounds massage your shoulders in a soft caress, allowing the tension in you to fall off.

Being here has made you grounded in yourself – you identify with your uniqueness, and your every step is a meditation about the fact that you are here and alive with days, months, and years ahead of you. And you can make anything of those days, months, and years. Anything really. You sigh at the future you see ahead of you, and you smile. You are not merely a survivor. You thrive. And in the days to come, you will thrive.

Much like the tall pine trees that surround you, your gaze cranes for your first sight of the reindeers in years. As you approach the forward-facing bench at the far end of your lawn, you are glad. You are glad that you have come here to find the benches vacant. But today, you are not content merely to sit and watch one reindeer. You long to see the majestic sight of all the reindeers at once.

And so, you take the long-winding stairs at the base of one tree. Ancient structures dot the park and lend to the already visible charm. Beautiful flowers envelop the railings you grasp for support as you climb patiently, one step at a time. You are not in any hurry. You get to the top of the building and walk to the balcony. There, you sink to the floor and allow yourself to connect to the essence of who you are. A brave and strong person who takes on feats and accomplishes them.

You sit calmly for a while and then get to your feet to take the view. And there, you are so taken by the sight you almost forget to breathe. Inhale. Exhale. It is all you can do not to soba the sight. Your heart is full of gratitude. One reindeer, Two, Three, Four. You count so many of them. And something about seeing such abundance in nature allows you to let a single tear go.

Your scalp begins to tingle, and you must listen as you take in this guide. Whatever it is that has bothered you, you are the answer. The answer has been in you all along – in your bravery, your courage, your ability to love, ability to carry on. You see it so much clearly now – how much of a force you are. How much of a presence you are and how much you will take on.

As you watch one graceful antler after another, you allow yourself to take in a big breath and let it out. You are here now. You are brave. You are strong. You know who you are.

SLED

In this small space, imagine that you are on a sled, a sled crafted to suit your tastes and whims. Your legs straddle both sides, and you anticipate the carefreeness of a joyful ride. It is only dawn, and you enjoy the quiet of the road as it is framed by the lushness and stillness of a snowy morning. Many are wrapped up in their homes at this time, but not you.

You have stepped outside for a time as this, to revel in the deep, orangey sky at this time. You have chosen to set out at this time, and you enjoy the experience of your town as the new day rises. You have the entire day ahead to enjoy this experience, and you smile as you take in the cool, intoxicating atmosphere around you. The gentle hum of a man's shed generator somewhere far away reminds you of Christmas mornings, where it seemed like anything could happen, and an adventure was always on the verge of being discovered. Here, it seems, you are limitless.

Your breath catches in expectance of the awe you are about to experience. What joy! What wonder! As your sled speeds onward, you imagine the footsteps that have once walked this path you now sled down. And you imagine the untold stories of these souls who have once walked this path. You are grateful for this opportunity for self-reflection and aloneness. As you continue in your sled, you pass by a home and stop at the sight of a child, hands cupped around his eyes, squinting through the glass of his living room at you. You are transfixed, such childlike wonder, such innocence. Only what seems like moments ago, you too have sat early on a Christmas morning, awake before your household, hands cupped around eyes and squinting at the world around you. You are transfixed at the sight, and soon, your own hands cup around your eyes, imitating the child before you can help it. You are at peace with yourself, at peace with the world.

You continue on your sledding journey as a foggy mist moves in slowly ahead. The lamp you hold in your arms now holds a dimmer light. A warmer light. You recall the advice of your friend as you set out on this morning – have a fun ride, she had called out. I will – you had returned. But now you find that you have not made this a wild ride. Instead, it has been a peaceful one. You have quietly moved down this town's slope. You feel a sense of inner peace and wisdom, one you haven't felt in a while, and you allow yourself to soak in it. Enjoy it.

Here, the burdens of the past do not matter. They fall away from around you like the shedding of a heavy blanket. You feel freer, lighter like fine gossamer print. You imagine this is what it feels like when honey melts in the mouth. Free. Light. Like the thousand winds that blow beneath the night sky. You are exactly where you need to be right now. Whatever has played out in your life thus far, welcome or unwelcome has led to this place. You are grateful to be here, and you can find acceptance for all that has come before. If one moment in the span of your entire life had played out differently, you would not be here. And you are glad to be here.

This day has given you a chance to begin again and start with a new, clean slate. You begin to feel yourself trust. Letting your inner intuition guide you, you take in the fragrance of the clean air and allow it to lead you. Where you are going, you do not know. The town, sparsely awake when you set out, is beginning to awaken. You pass a woman blowing warm air into her hands. She pauses, rubs her hands together, and blows into them again to stay warm. You had wished not to see anyone on this path, but now you are glad you have.

As you pass by her, she gives out a friendly smile, and your heart spins at the pleasantness of her face. You know that this is as much self-care for her as it is for her. You feel blessed, fortunate to have met another traveler on this self-love journey. You do not know what has brought her here, but you are glad she is here. You are both content and you know that your life is bigger and greater than your attempts to control every part of your day. You feel relief as you surrender to the limitless potential, to the possibilities of the greater good. You surrender to the flow, and in this moment, you feel a fullness of joy.

You stop your sled and bend to allow your fingers to dance through the snow. You let it sift through your hands and experience the coolness in your fingers. You glance around again and the stillness in the air reminds you to get going. You hug your arms around you, enjoying the gentle massage, and get back on the sled. It has been a fulfilling morning for you, a reminder to let go of worries, fears, and concerns, to move on with grace and strength.

You yawn as a wave of tiredness comes upon you. But a peaceful tiredness, a lazy one that does not hold pressure or place a demand on you. You are still and content as you begin your journey home. You remember to stare and notice as you continue home. You notice the contrast of red doors against the white of the snow, and you view with bafflement the swirls of purple, blue, and soft greens that your neighbor has spread on her clothesline.

On the property where you stay, you park the sled outside and walk to the door, climbing up your grey-colored stairs, stopping only to remove articles of clothing originally designed to keep you warm. You cannot suppress the smile that forms on your lips as you take the stairs, two at a time. You feel truly a leap of joy in your heart, a surge of peace. You are overwhelmed by love for yourself and this moment.

On a whim, you walk slowly down the stairs again to observe the sled that has bestowed you this experience. You run your hands along it, feel the chipped paint underneath your hands, and wonder how many other people it has humbled with the gift of a snowy experience. You remind yourself to pick up paint for it the next time you visit the store.

You return to your room, and with a soft drowsy smile, you drop off to sleep.

POLAR BEAR

Tonight, we journey into the lands of the polar bears. You may consider this voice as Cuddle up and find a safe, comfortable place where you may drift away and gradually cross the bridge into dreamland. There may have been times in your life where you imagined how wonderful it would be to journey into an unknown land. A strange place you have never been before now. Tonight, you'll find yourself safely encapsulated in a snow bubble and have a sleep adventure from which you can observe the world of the polar bears.

This is a safe protective bubble. With the walls around you, you are enclosed away from worries, and you are free to let go, right now. You are well. You are loved. And you are free to let go. Inhale deeply as your belly rises, and your lungs expand to take in air. Now, let all the air out in a soft exhalation. You are free to empty out all your fears, just sighing it out, how good it is to release all that tension. You may even allow that sigh turn into a yawn and just enjoy that yawn. You may sigh and yawn all you want, without restraint. Simply give your body all the signs that you are ready to descend into sleep.

Inhale for three, two, and one. And exhale for three, two, and one.

As you do, visualize you are walking along the edge of the road. Inhale the crisp air and exhale that air from your mouth. Watch as the warmth of your mouth releases the air in a cold huff. You can feel the stillness of the town behind you as you walk along this edge of the town. Enjoy the stillness and feel it blossom into deep quiet solitude. The air smells of nothing. As you walk along the shoulder of a barely used street, notice the stark contrast of the townsfolk's colors of magenta, chartreuse as the trees near the readiness of letting go. Just as right now, you are ready to let go of anything that weighs you down. Anything that you do not want to accompany you on this trip you are about to embark on.

Take another deep breath and allow yourself to journey to your childhood, to the first time you ever saw your own breath, how you did it again, and again until you felt like you were smoking. Inhale. Exhale. Inhale. Exhale. You walk this path again and your feet, snuggled in warm socks and boots steps on the clean whiteness of the night snow.

You want to make a return to your cabin but pause. Your inner voice leads you in a different direction. You see the flurries of the snowfall, melting as they kiss the ground, some even melting before they hug the floors. It is an amazing sight. You pass the turn to your house and follow the bend to another turn. It is now damp beneath your boots, and a cooler wind begins to blow as the air changes from crisp to slightly windy.

Warm your hands against the soft flannel of your shirt and let your thoughts wander, not settling on anything. You startle as a family of deer walk across, and your eyes watch them in awe of the simplicity with which you have stumbled on such sight. You note your happiness and is humbled to be considered worthy of viewing such a sight. You know that you are deserving of such beauty. Such beauty.

You walk on for a while, not stopping to check how far you have come. Instead, you focus on the drops of snow lakes, the contrast of your brown boots against the white of the snow and the clarity of your breath as you exhale. Inhale. Exhale.

The polar bear stops, and you are caught in a direct gaze. Slowly, it turns, and you begin to follow slowly, unsure as it winds through the snowy island. You wonder if you have dreamt this up, but the stark whiteness of its fur lends a reality to it that is distinctly un-dreamlike. Its largeness baffles you even as you enjoy its slow gait across the land. One foot in front of the other, you shuffle behind it, following wherever it takes you. The simplicity of it frees you – you have only one job tonight, to follow and it is a pleasant job.

You do not have to think about anything – only to walk slowly behind, and this frees you to follow and explore your thoughts. You examine each one, accepting it, and let it go like the melting of a snowflake. One thought and then another and then another and then another. It is a peaceful evening.

Suddenly, the polar bear stops, and you are brought to a halt as well. It rises on its hind limbs and stops as though to stare at you, and in them, you see the wisdom of your years reflected at you. You remind yourself of how wise you are, how many transitions, and challenges in your life you have forged through and triumphed over. You know of the strength of the polar bear and are convinced in this moment of your strength as well. As you meditate on this, all harmful thoughts that do not serve you are allowed to escape into the night air. Take the time to appreciate the gentle shift in your energy, from just a few minutes ago. How peaceful and calm your mind is now.

Deep within, you feel a grounded stillness – calm at ease. A warm glow of appreciation surrounds you for the bucolic beauty that surrounds you on this journey. You have stopped for a while, but you only now notice, allowing yourself to savor this moment. You feel warm – almost too warm even, and it is all you can do to break out into joyous laughter. Peace surrounds you. Peace encloses you. You are wrapped snuggly in this peace.

You feel the soft fabric of your scarf tickle your face as you continue in the serenity of this night. You inhale the fresh air and cock your ear for any sounds. There are no sounds. It is still and calm in the world tonight. You remember your distant companion, the polar bear, and look up, but he is no longer there. You feel a sense of relief, this solitude is something you have been seeking, and here it is – all for you right now. The air so clean and fresh makes you feel so festive as you inhale and exhale.

You feel the cold wind shifting against your face, and you decide that rather than return to your home, you will continue this invigorating walk for a while. Your lungs fill with the cold air, and you are compelled to run and dance along the way. You focus all of your energy on this mind-tingling energy of being alive, of being present to witness that. you smile in gratitude that this is all yours right now. Laughter escapes your snow-kissed lips, almost shattering the silence. You realize that you could do anything here- you could lay against the down to feel the snow against you, and you could dance and run around in circles.

You are ready to head home now, feeling fulfilled as tiredness takes over. Your body suddenly feels heavy and ready to let go. Your mind counts the steps as you go up to your room. One, two, three, four, five – you turn the knob of your room. There, you take off your winter layers and let your cool toes find warmth within your plush slippers. You sink into your bed, and there you drift away to dreamland where you dream of friendly, companionable polar bears.

SEALS

Fall asleep in this story as you dive under the deep waters of serenity. Like being under a thick blanket, there is a stillness, a solitude that offers you distance from the madness and noise of your waking life. You may go deeper and deeper into this aquatic escape where peace is as abundant as the water itself. There is no room for anything but self-love, self-care, and the nourishing of your body and mind and spirit here before you drift to sleep.

Burrow under the sheets for restoration and a good night's sleep for every night for the rest of your life. Use this time too, with your mind embellish so that these words may take you wherever you want to go. And as you read, you may let go of yourself and fall into sleep. Get comfortable in your bed as you sink deeper and deeper down as you inhale like the crest of a wave.

Notice the feeling of hydration in your own body right now and pay attention to the gentle flow of your life force so that the ocean feels welcoming as it beckons to you. You may visualize the flapping of the waves and the feeling of your feet stepping upon the metallic blue of the ocean's sandy shores. Above you, it is a starry, starry night, and the sky is a cooling shade of velvet black.

The salty seashore reaches your toes as the waves crash again and again over your feet. You realize that this moment, like many other moments in our lives, is only temporary. This place is for tranquillity, and in this moment, you feel a distinct peace so real you feel you could trap it in a bottle. Beyond you, a family of seals play ons hore, and you watch the water glisten on their bodies as they move one, two, three in ocean-like movements.

You pocket this sliver of time as a memory you will remember even in your waking moments. You are entranced by the black of the night, and soon, your eyes begin to droop as you allow the soft sounds of the ocean waves carry you to sleep.

Chapter Three:
Stories Of The Jungle

TROPICAL RAIN FOREST

Nested within a forest, a composition of beautiful scenery, exquisite sounds, and an array of beauty was the habitation of a group of people. People bound by love, connected by blood, and lived based on trust. They can be considered and be said to be living off the grid, completely far from everyone, on the outskirts and away from modern civilization. Choosing to live incommunicado and finding solace in the arms of nature. Tracing the steps back to their primordial roots, they dined and wined with the forces of nature. They lived their lives to the fullest, avoiding the daily grind, the hustle and bustle of the metropolis, the pollution of the urban centers, and the noise of residential areas. The world in the forest is one that is peaceful, indirect contact with nature. And environment where there was an abundance of everything one ever needed. A compendium of symphonies can be heard by day, while soothing, relaxing tones can be heard at night.

The forest, a place of humble abode, a place where one can hear his or her thoughts explicitly. In the middle of all this peace, there dwelled two of the world's most notorious and deviant minds.

They devised a plan to steal the most precious thing belonging to all the forests of the world, the eye of the panther. The eye of the panther is very similar to the heart of any living thing, the life-giving organ, the organ that ensures the continuity of life. The eye of the panther would be expected to be a huge piece of gold, shaped into a ball. Rather, it is a blue-colored jewel with two distinct lines coming from the top to the bottom of it. On it was inscribed the name of the goddess of the forests. Her name no one knew, but often time, prayer and offerings were offered in honor of her. Without the eye of the panther in its rightful position, everything would be in a state... A state no one ever wished would come.

However, these two despite knowing they weren't meant to even conceive such an idea in their hearts at first went to the heart of the jungle, through the streams and the oceans, down the cliffs and around the valleys, riding the waves and flowing along the treacherous rapids plucked out the forest's jewel. They literally removed the heart of the jungle. The life-giving force that was encapsulated in the blue jewel in the eye of the panther, which was located on the ridge of Olympia, had been removed.

They turned the forest to a flaming region; it was as though an apocalypse had begun. Lightning and thunder, earthquakes and tremors, fire and brimstone rained down on the forests of the world. The goddess had unleashed her wrath as her heart had been stolen by some miscreants. Rains seized, and the droughts rolled in majestically. The grains of the fields tuned to ash, and smoke plummeted from within. Jaayla and Markel had done evil. They had awoken the fury of the goddess.

Sipping on coconut juice and enjoying themselves, the two men discussed and rejoiced about the havoc they had caused over the world. They joked and laughed about how they should be recognized as world powers since they held the key to putting an end to the world's misery.

Peace had seized all over the world, and a worldwide manhunt began for the two most wanted criminals in the universe at that time. The forest, which has always been known for its grilling rigidities even without the present chaos and disasters, it's unpredictable, volatile, and dangerous nature has now made everywhere inhabitable, and many people fled to the seas for comfort, with the Sea becoming a haven for people.

A haven that only spans over a particular region and has jurisdiction only within a specific region. It is not an international standard for safety. So if any inhabitants of the safe-haven now the seas should step out, such individuals would be left to face and deal with the impulses and problems that the goddess fires at such person.

This was the case for the two miscreants, Jaayla and Markel, after being drunk with wine and under the influence. They stepped out of their haven, they wanted to see and feel what the new world felt like. Wanting to know what was on the other side of the curtain of peace the experienced in their place of abode, they wanted to explore. Go far, explore the treacherous depths of the world, give meaning to all her dimensions. Little did they know that their past would catch up to them so fast. The grievous thing they had done in times past were just at their heels.

All the havoc caused to nature, the deforestation, global warming, river pollutions, famines, drought, the ravaging plagues, and all evils and putting safe havens, the very element that house nature completely and in her true form all around the globe at risk of extinction. So with these, people who were already on a manhunt for them, found and caught them in the act as they were about robbing another precious jewel.

Upon catching them, they were taken to court, made to present the eye of the panther, and all other precious jewels which were illegally in their possession. So many things was discovered, and they were rightly tried and sentenced to the dungeons of Zeus.

The fruits of our labor of the world soldiers were soon seen. The green leaves of the forests return to their original state, animals exclaiming loudly under the canopy of the trees. We can see a rejuvenation of life in the forest.

How good is the feeling of restoration? The jewel was restored by Amazonia, the leader of the 12th battalion of conservationists. Equilibrium was reset, and balance is once again restored to the environment. The forest is back on her feet, a safe haven for all.

RIVERS

So many beauties exist in this world of ours, so many things that can bring joy to individuals and organisms living and co-habiting on the surface of the earth. We have several mountains, plateaus, hills, ridges, oceans, and seas. But one that catches the attention strikingly is the river called emerald. Her beauty, the energy, the majesty, and the grace all encapsulated in one body of water, finding her course through the land with confidence.

Roaring and snaking around the hills was the mighty and great river emerald. It was majestic as it was the singular river that gave birth to so many tributaries and also wet the environment. At its peak, her voice can be heard miles away, thrashing and banging into the sides of the rocks that are in her way.

Emerald had a sparkle when called to life could be seen in her. She carried various lives, and so many things depended on River emerald, without her is drought, without her spamming, without her the low Green and beautiful flowers in the valleys would be absent. She was a force to be reckoned with, the great on mighty real.

But soon disaster hits, there is chaos in the land. River emerald is drying up, the rains were held back, the sun increased its intensity, and nothing seemed to be working well. The Waters of the deep was refraining while the oceans were silent. Lush greens of the valleys, the beautiful flowers the majestic trees all became like a skeletal frame of a starved mouse.

The tributaries dried up, emerald grew quiet, farming ceased, and famine took over. Nothing seemed to be in equilibrium; it was as though the world had shifted off its axis, and Earth had been shaken to her very foundation. But as we all know or have experienced time to time, no bad situation lasts forever. Darkness only is for a while; the sun has its appointed time to rise. The moon her time to glow and the stars their time to shine. A friend will always come to our aid. A family will have compassion and run to our rescue. So was the case for emerald. Her glow was missed, her roars cherished, the valleys grew too silent, and the groaning of people excited.

A huge god stooped to meet river emerald. The river, once mighty, pushing through every crevice and opening, now meandered through the sand and dreamt of the sea. The god spoke to her with the voice of the ancients — "Let me help you roar again." The god made it rain endlessly for time. Minutes turned into hours, hours turned into days, days into weeks, and weeks into months till the very last cloud was gone. The river swelled and gained her pride back. But along with the clouds, the god lost his voice.

Months then rolled by. Now the summer scorched. The sun relentlessly beat the river, dried up the deep, and left the hungry sand with no choice but to eat up the dwindling river.

The river didn't die, though, a very resilient river. Silently, she found her way and flowed beneath the sand, beneath the rocky mounds, on which she unleashed her fury in past times, in and out of caves where bats slept all day. She birthed millions of ferns, figs, and shrubs that thrived in the dark. The god didn't know what to do concerning the issue at hand. But being a very wise god and one desperate to save this river that had captured his heart, he left his throne behind and broke off the crown of a huge iceberg and sent the largest glacier down. It rained ice! The glacier coming down from a height that is indescribable, formed a furious stream. A stream that was never going to be at the mercies of the sun, the scorching heat produced by the sun, or any other force of nature that can threaten her existence.

The glacier could be seen plummeting down with only one purpose; rejuvenation. And it sure did accomplish the purpose for which it was sent.

Nourished forever, the river flourished forever. She flooded the caves with power, wet the valleys with perfection, and restored beauty and balance, the plains were made whole again. She also met the faraway sea. Mangrove forests soon lined her banks. Balance was restored back to the land. River emerald's smile every time the sun was overhead was always a sight to behold.

After all the help the god proffered, he went back to his humble abode and smiled constantly as he saw something great that he had been able to achieve. He saw hope, he saw joy, and that made him happy. Also, as a token of appreciation to the god, emerald always gives a tenth of all life in her to the god's court. Fishes, eels, crabs, amongst other things.

PARROTS ECHOED

Chirp! Chirp! The birds sang, their sounds bounced off the walls, echoing with such symphony and grace. Effortless in capturing the attention of the onlookers and drawing them closer. I listened to the blend of sounds and the delivery of such. The sounds spoke to me, sent a message into the depths of my soul, resonating within me, and stirring up passion and excellence. Their echoes soothing and relieving. Also, it was backed with the very essence that eased my stress.

Oh! How splendid these parrots looked, the elegant patterns that spoke with depth. How majestic they are in their own little way. But paying more rapt attention, I could see that the echoes were as a result of a parrot being stuck in a situation, frantically trying to rescue and help one of its own. I watched from a distance, from the window of my little hut on the other end of the jungle. The songs seemed to be fading in and out. Then as I took a deeper look, I saw a sight that made me smile.

A spotted animal, which walked with ease and ran faster than any other animal in the kingdom had witnessed the crimes of one of the tyrannical snakes in the kingdom first hand, was set to stand before the whole jungle as a witness. But he was just a toddler, a young one. Due to the peculiarity and sensitivity of the case, she had to be transported in the best animal convoy ever to where happened to be a fort Knox room. A room that was completely sealed and no slithering, crawling, gnarling, or roaring animal could get into. Moreover, the location is unknown to any soul in the jungle except the top leaders. From the room, a live message was to be broadcast straight to the congress hall. This was done in order to protect the high priced witness. I saw a great number of guard dogs, well-trained horses, and an army of ostriches all for the purpose of protecting "the package." She was very beautiful, majestic, and well looking.

So, the standard procedure is that an animal brings the equipment to be used for the live feed. The elegant couriers in past times are not known by the inhabitants. But we know the animal always happens to be a fast, strong muscular animal, one that would be able to maneuver his way through the jungle with minimal interruptions. The animal that is never challenged to a race, the whispers on the streets said. Their maneuvering skills are top-notch, the accuracy, none can beat, even the beauty, only a few can stand up to it. But little did anyone know amongst the general populace of the jungle that the convoy had been compromised. ADT 1 (Animal Delta Team 1) had been compromised.

On getting to the Haven, "Fort Knox," the place for the live transmission, one of the ostrich, the head of the whole operations checked in the courier who brought in the equipment for the broadcast. After the courier was checked and the package delivered, one of the security escorts was asked to lead her out, but upon reaching the door, the fellow pushed the courier into another room. She was searched, and all means by which she could communicate with other animals were seized immediately. She protested, what are you doing? She asked, but she was shot 9 different times. She collapsed to the floor, consequently, the setup for the broadcast is complete, and the process initiated.

The key was slotted into the hole, and the connection was established. Immediately, like lightning and thunder, a green-colored gas filled up the whole room. The gas is called ENXOME. Enxome happens to be a naturally occurring gas in the animal kingdom. A liquid extracted from the leaves and the stalk of the kwayakwaya tree. It is then changed to the gaseous state. The gas was released, and it always has the same effect on everyone, like cyanide to humans. But this has a different effect; it puts them straight into a comatose state. Reason why the gas is usually kept in vaults hidden in the mountains with the elders being the ones to possess the copy of the map per time. The rogue cop then proceeded to get a gas mask to escape since he presumed that everyone in the room was already in the induced comatose state. But little did he know the courier had a kamanon, and this prevented the penetration of the bullets into the heart.

The courier stood up and clawed at the ostrich's face. Stomping and leaving a permanent indentation on the beak. But all this was the beginning of the whole story. Due to compassion, the courier grabbed the witness on his way out. The witness who happened to be in shock due to the fast-paced cataclysmic events that surrounded him momentarily did not want to follow the courier. The courier grabbed him again and said, "let's leave! Your life is in danger, and if you do not leave now, something else might happen. The whole team has been compromised, and I'm the only one you can trust."

A pure soul, one filled with compassion she backed him, and they flew.

But as they were about exiting the already compromised area, a troop of men was seen opening the gate, and their motives were well written on their faces. Hunt them down, we saw. A full-blown attempted murder was in process.

Wow, what a wonderful story! My name is Adler, a parrot, and my owner has taught me a wide variety of words, phrases. And due to my well-developed brain, I've been able to write books of my own. Surprising right? Yup! Yup!! Yup!!! I also have a parrot voice, so… you can imagine how I'm talking also!

Skrrrrrrrrrrrrrrrrrrrrrrrrrrrrrrrrrrrrrrrrrrrrrrrrrrrrrrrrrrrrrrrr!

You'll be surprised how much I know about you humans as well. Bye!

BIG TREES

Many years ago, Bambi always thought Himself to be the best because only Him and just a few others had that unique feature that attracted human beings and brought a lot of attention. He would mockingly tell Shifa to add more weight because He was too slim, so he might die soon. "You're a man and men ought to be bigger than this, slim" He would always ring daily in his head. At first, Shifa always laughed about it, but when he saw that his brothers were beginning to get bothered and saddened by the mockful assertions, Bambi made to all of them, he cried and condemned himself for being so slim yet so tall. "No one comes close; I rarely get any attention from anyone. Am I really that bad?" went through his mind daily. He always blamed the gods for allowing him to have such exquisite height but so bony, hence looking so unattractive.

Many times, because of how He and his family appeared, one of his brothers had been taken away captive to be used in forced labor somewhere unknown to the rest of them. Not only that, his brother, his younger sister, and mum, had to undergo such a difficult situation as well. Therefore, everyone lived in fear of when they would be kidnapped, taken away from their loved ones. So, for Shifa's family, every day was a day they were expecting to be taken away from their loved ones.

Such a life of negative expectations and fear! And Bambi, who on the other end kept reminding him of this predicament, didn't make the matter better at all.

Bambi was a tall, wide, and full green tree that always provided shades for people from sun and rain while Shifa was very tall but was not wide enough to provide any shades for humans.

What the trees used to compete with one another was the amount of attention they got from humans, and so imagine how Shifa and his family always felt all day, all week, all month and all year long! They simply never stood a chance to be outstanding among the trees because virtually no humans came close.

In fact; many times, the government would order that trees of such nature as Shifa be cut down for their industrial use. So, all the wide and tall trees which were referred to as the big trees had all it took; they attracted human attention while the tall and slim trees attracted more eyes of people looking to fell trees for various purposes.

Over the months, Shifa seemed to be among the last survivors. He lived a life of sorrow because he could not predict what would happen tomorrow and could not become like Bambi overnight.

Shifa had made so many prayers such that the gods finally could not stand the bitterness of his heart and for his remaining family. The gods decided to react in a way that would spur equilibrium.

Early the next day, Bambi noticed Shifa looking very different. Shifa was all of a sudden looking as full as the rest.

 Obviously, Shifa had just been groomed by the gods, and not only did Shifa escape death, she also attracted much more attention from humans. Therefore, till date, the bambi and Shifa never relate because although Shifa is an open hearted beauty, Bambi did not like the god's idea of making tall and slim trees wide. He did not want so many people to be referred to as big trees. However, having no control over the situation, he struggled for weeks to accept it but later got to.

The most difficult times were when He had to watch his regular visitors stare at Him and then walk right past to Shifa and his family.

Shifa, however, was always good from the onset and never mocked Bambi, knowing and coming to agree that the sky is large enough for everyone to fly!

TRIBU

"Good morning class, we have two new students joining us today," said Mrs. Brad as the students of Hazal college made a noise in their classroom.

"Hi, my name is stresan, I love to put people on the edge and many times I am inconsiderate, but we just might get along. I'm just being honest about how I am!" Said the first new student who got booed by the whole class when he gave such an introduction. "Put people on the edge? Inconsiderate? You can't stay in our class then!" murmured the students all over the large spaced class, which had just 20 tables and chairs for students studying metaphysics.

After the little uproar Stresan had caused, the second student was asked to introduce herself. It was so obvious she was more of a quiet, calm person. Sweetly, she said, "I'm Yogen, it's nice to meet you, everyone, you'd have delight knowing me better, trust me." Everyone cheered, especially because of that innocent kind of smile she had.

Hazal college was barely five years old existent, so each course had just a little number of students available, and one trend that was noticeable among the students was only new students got along with each other.

One time, a red hair called Steve joined in and actually kept walking alone until a new class member came along six months later. The remaining classmates already created unbreakable groups that they just always frowned at receiving anyone new. The whole students in the school were patterned like that, so if anyone came, they decided to be hostile and just keep to their "groups," that person would have to wait for another newbie student or the person was lucky if a student was to join in at the same time.

This was the case of Stresan and Yogen. Even though Yogen would have preferred to have a female friend, stresan was Male, and she just had to get used to that, so she doesn't walk alone all her years in college.

At lunchtime, Stresan approached Yogen and started a conversation. "Hi," he said, admiring how cute she was. "Hello, can we make proper introductions now, not all that bulldog stuff you said in the class" Yogen replied, and Stresan immediately started laughing. "Okay, fine, I am stresan, everyone calls me stress because I actually like to get people on the edge and leave them tired every time I meet them." Stresan said. Yogen looked at the expression on his face and seeing that He actually was not smiling, knew that he was not joking about the introduction. Although she wondered but she just introduced herself in like manner as He did.

"I'm yogen, widely called Yoga, I help people have a touch with their inner mind, and I aid relaxation every time."

"Really!" Stresan said, "That's like the direct opposite of me, I definitely want to know you better." Yogen replied, "we would know each other better; the next class seems to be canceled, so I actually don't mind talking right now, so tell me all about you!"

They smiled at each other and sipped some water just before the conversation continued.

"My real name is Stress Nosleep, but because of how people hated me, I had to start calling myself Stresan. I uncontrollably put people under tension, weary them out. Even though I am a normal part of people's lives, many times, I am spoken against by doctors, health workers. People are always advised to get rid of me. I have gone to various schools and tried to make friends but before I know, whoever gets along with me does so for only about two weeks max before they start getting strict advises to stay off me if they don't want to regret it. That's the kind of life I have lived thus far! I've tried to be in a relationship several times, but all have failed. One time, I dated a girl named Anger, and we seemed to be the worst combination just from the third day of dating! Other girls have just outrightly told me no. Finding someone who gets me and can get other people to love me as well has been my greatest desire for so many years now. How about you, tell me about yourself."

"That's a lot to be going on with just one person, I am really sorry about all that you've had to go through. I'm yogen, original name is Yoga Relief. People love me and talk to me when they want to get some physical and health well-being. I teach people wellness all round. Everywhere I go, I get introduced, I see people flocking all around me trying to say hi and ask if we could be friends. Truth is I am actually a relief to people who are worked up or have undergone a lot of activities and just need to chill out. I have different ways I do this. Primarily, I teach them to relax their body, relax their mind, understand how their mind works, develop a connection between their body and mind and how to release emotional energy. I teach them various ways they can achieve this. Then, I encourage them to practice all I have thought as often as they can, and because my prescriptions have always worked, more people flock around me and want to talk to me. So, the truth is I can't really relate with how your life has been because mine has been the direct opposite. But, I do think we would be best of friends, we complement one another, and your weakness is my strength. Whatcha think?"

Stresan was speechless; he had never heard or seen someone as delightful as Yogen. He already liked her! He felt there was a connection he had with her that he had never had with anyone. He thought that if perhaps over time he gets her to date him and then marries him, even if people shut him out, his wife would be there to help him get relieved of all that hurt. And oh well, when people shut Him out, He could just as well introduce his wife to them and in that way get to be loved by them since he gave them an easy way out.

Stresan looked forward to spending more time with Yogen. "If only I get her to be mine, then I myself would have a way to relieve myself when I feel bad because of how people treat me."

While he was lost in his thoughts, Yogen told him it was time for their next class. So, the two new friends picked up their bags and went for their class.

MONKEYS

"I don't know if I really want to go on this trip, I'd just rather stay home and prepare for dad's birthday." Said Charlotte, the daughter of Mr. Sarfs, the wealthiest man in Florida.

"That's a silly excuse, party planners are on the edge for that already. Come on girl, let's go. Remember, it's our last year here, spending any extracurricular time with our friends and classmates wouldn't be bad." Anna persuasively told her best friend since kindergarten.

The medal high school had a camping trip for the finalists, and this especially was a time for various parents and guardians to show off their wealth starting from the Parent-teacher forum meetings to the sports day and then finally to the camp facilities sponsorship.

Charlotte Sarfs's dad was a billionaire, highly reputable for his four-star hotels in strategic places in Florida. Her dad was one to show off his wealth and let everyone know He was proud of his daughter. On the other hand, Charlotte was an indoor kind of person, even though she had all she needed provided for her, she was very weird and loved to keep to herself. Everyone complained about how unpredictable she always was; especially in her reactions, her sense of humor, you just cannot say how she would react to certain things, for this reason, Anna, her best friend, was the only one who stuck around her.

Many students tried to be close to her because of her dad's status, but when they saw she really wasn't that kind of a spoilt brat, show off money kind of fellow, they had rethinks.

One thing that was very noticeable about her was her love for animals. Oh, Charlotte could stay in her room with her dog all day and scarcely speak to any human; she was getting better as she advanced in age anyway. When she was a child, she hated anyone carrying her or too many people around. What a strange little girl she was!

Over the weeks, when the camp trip was announced, she didn't even give it any thoughts; she already made up her mind not to be involved in such activities, more especially since she wasn't allowed to bring her dog because it was a time of human bonding as the principal said. That on its own was a double no for her! Charlotte to be separated from her dog? From her dear Max? No way!

Anna didn't let her be until she agreed to join in for the trip. "You are my best friend, I need you there," she constantly said until she finally got Charlotte to reluctantly agree. "Since you have debunked all my excuses, fine then, I would come, only if you help me pack, I'm lazy." "Of course!!!!," screamed excited Anna. Finally, she got her best friend to agree.

A few days down the line, the morning of the day the medal finalists was to set out finally came. Anna had slept over at Charlotte's and was so excited. The girls got ready and got to school to join the bus, which was going quite some miles away to a resort center.

At about 1 pm, the bus arrived at Malago resort center. Everyone was so excited except Charlotte; she couldn't wait to be given their room keys so she would disappear from everyone's presence. Just as her dream finally came to pass, while she passed by in the lobby, she saw her greatest weakness stare at her from some miles away. It was an animal! Charlotte took steps back to see what animal it was exactly as she leaped for joy within. It was a monkey! "This wouldn't be as bad as I thought, you know." She thought to herself. Just when she was very close to having a closer view of the monkey, she saw the resort center workers come in a haste to take the monkey away, they said the monkeys stayed at the other end of the compound but that Lala which was the monkey's name sort of escaped. Charlotte and the monkey had jammed eyes, and the monkey was already stretching her hands to shake Charlotte. There was no way she would allow them take her back!

As expected, Charlotte pleaded with the workers to please allow the monkey to stay with her the three days they would be guests at their resort center. They disagreed over and over, but after so many pleas and so much convincing, they grudgingly agreed. "You know this is not allowed legally, right?" They asked, but she said, "I promise nothing would go wrong."

The workers knew they had to keep it a secret from the director who might not notice unless told, so they all agreed to do so.

Just as guessed, everywhere Chatlotte went, her new made friend Lala went with her. Even though Charlotte knew about how it was risky having a monkey as a pet and all that restriction, she couldn't resist Lala. This particular one seemed really calm to her, "what could she possibly do wrong?" "Just look at this gorgeous albino" constantly ran through her mind, and in three days, she got attached to Lala as a mother gets attached to her child over months.

She had already been telling Anna how she was going to ask to buy Lala to take back home. But Anna, who knew much about animal laws, kept telling her the reality which of course she didn't want to agree to. The truth remained that Lala was a monkey, and these animals are wild and cannot be made domestic pets, but Lala just felt something could be done for her to keep it.

She was well aware of the kind of habitat that they would rather be in, and she was sure her dad could easily ask for that to be built. Rather slowly, the three days finally were spent, and the bus was to leave on the evening of the third day. Knowing the possibility of Lala being dropped, Charlotte went to the director's office early enough in the afternoon and laid out her desires not only putting the workers in trouble because they had actually let a monkey stay in a guest's custody but putting the director off guard as well because it simply wasn't the right time to bring up such "impossible" matters.

"First of all, it is banned according to the law; monkeys cannot be domesticated, and then this is the only albino monkey left in this area, there's no way the authority would let her go, no matter what happens. So, young lady quit bothering me." He said. "Do you know whose daughter I am? I am the daughter to Mr. Sarfs! My dad would provide the perfect habitat, every precaution needed to be taken, just please let her go" pleaded Charlotte, but when it was obvious, her desires won't be met, she left his office greatly sorrowful, and just about twenty minutes later some of the workers came to take Lala back.

Of course, Charlotte was broken, but she was not one to pour out her emotions so easily. The bus left at about 4:15, and the memories of her moments with Lala stuck on her mind all through.

On getting to school, the next Monday, a finalist had to volunteer to talk to the whole school about their experience at the camp trip. Charlotte raised her hand tall, and of course, everyone was astonished. "What would she possibly say?" they all wondered.

"I know for humans' safety, many rules are laid out, but I feel there should always be an exception. Lala was sweet, reasonable, and in no way can cause harm or detrimental effects in a home. I know monkeys are wild, but I wish they would have just given it another thought..." Charlotte said and in the middle started sobbing.

The whole students were astonished and felt empathetic because of her passion, while some just felt "all rich kids get spoilt, some just do really stupid things, crying for a monkey barely met three days?"

Well, one thing was certain, if monkeys actually have emotions, then Lala was definitely as hurt as Charlotte was!

Chapter Four:
Stories of Tropical Islands

Atollo

Hello there, my name is John. I used to be a very stressed out person. Ever since the age of nine, my parents decided that I had a multiple personality disorder. They were saying that because I was always moody and tired. It seemed as though something or someone else might have been living inside of me. Little did they know that this was because they were separated. The separation really stressed me out and made me create someone to protect myself from the stress caused by it. However, recently, it had gotten worse now. I am twenty-two years old, in college, and studying for my master's degree in physics.

Yes, it is the time of the year when I have to prepare for my exams. This year was a particularly stressful year for me, especially with the lecturers demanding short deadlines and lots of assignments. This really got me stressed. I was so stressed that I couldn't even sleep at all. Eventually, I was beginning to show signs of insomnia as my stress levels got extremely high. Ultimately, my diverse personalities kicked in. One of my personalities shows evidence of madness while the other shows evidence of anger then one day, my friend, Jane, got really concerned about my multiple personalities resulting from my stress levels, and she suggested I sought help. To do this, I had to go very far, and that's where I met a meditation teacher on a tropical island in the Maldives. The name of the island was Atollo.

This island was very beautiful, and the wind blew all so soft and made me feel life and the reinvigorating aspects of life. The sea shore's water redirected the sun's extraordinary glare at me and is compelled to turn away towards an ever-growing vine jungle, trees, and murkiness. The trees making an overhang of the wilderness concealing what lies underneath. There is no dense of a creepy-crawly, winged animal or reptile, no call of a human voice, just the consistent rhythmical lap of the ocean. The sound of the ocean makes him shudder with dread for what could be lying in the wilderness.

As I stroll through the wilderness, my mental fortitude is raised by the light, which streams through the covering illuminating the wonders of the wilderness and I stopped to smell the blossoms and look at things, which I never thought existed.

I prevent myself from getting occupied and focus on my reason for coming here. I cleared my path through the wilderness, chopping down vines and leaves in my way, attempting to discover a conclusion to this unending wilderness. Similarly, as I was going to abandon my mission, I saw a light not very far up ahead and race for it.

In the evenings, you would see the trees move rhythmically as though the wind was playing a musical tune to them. They danced all so easily and made me also want to dance. And as I continued staring at the beauty of this place, I met the meditation teacher, who then gave me something very simple to do to calm my stress. It was then I realized that the solution to all of life's troubles lies in the simple things of life. The most important things in life are the basic things. He said that every evening, I should go for a walk around the island. He said I should do this every evening around 9:30 for about 3 hours.

Seeing that I work majorly at night, it was quite easy for me to do. So, as I walked around the island and listened to the beautiful gems of the wind, my mind became much calmer, and I became much more mindful.

Doing this the first night, I assumed that I slept more peacefully because I was tired from walking around the island. I continued the next day and the day after and the day after that and then I realized I wasn't tired, I was actually just calm and relaxed from moving around in a calm environment.

I decide to do one more activity. The next time I went, I took my pocket knife along with me on my now regular evening strolls, and I decided to carve and write songs and poems into the trees this was very relaxing. It helped me realize that the little things of life, the things that we seemingly ignore, the beauty of the trees, the wonder of the traffic, the colors of humanity, and things like this. I did this much more regularly, and eventually, my stress levels became very low.

This, new routine, did not only reduce my stress levels but also helped to satisfy my multiple personalities. Each personality came out but was never in a bad mood. They were all happy and satisfied.

Going back to college, I decided to carry out this activity continually. Every evening, by 9:00 pm, I would go to the college fountain and take a stroll imagining myself still in the Atollo island. This tropical island was it for me, it made me very relaxed, and sleep was now much easier to come across.

MY SUMMER WITH PALMS

I remembered when daddy came in with the news about our vacation for the summer. He had prepared our minds so much that we anticipated the travel, as though it was possible to travel ahead of time. We still had 3weeks before the breaks. Our hearts were so fixed on the mountain town of Salento in Central Columbia.

We have had stories about how nature screams in Cocora valley. From the giant palm trees to the hummingbirds and streams that flow through the jungle. A lovely sight to behold.

Daddy told us stories about the memories he had shared with his friends in his high school days when they went for an excursion. He always speaks with this very wild smile on his lips as he says, "these stories are ever fresh like it was yesterday". Daddy was never given opportunities to always go a distance from his parents. When he was in school, he was always under a close watch of his teachers and students rarely played with him because of his health conditions. When his Geography teacher spoke about this excursion, he had seen it as an opportunity to do things he was never opportune to do. He had made plans with his teacher who loves and has always had compassion for him to do anything possible to go on this trip. He had made plans with friends on how they were going to have fun like it was going to be his last. Daddy said he had actually thought that these days might actually be his last because he had always lived with the fear that if he ever stayed far from his parents for days, he might never survive it. He swore to himself that if these days were going to be his last days, he must make it his best last.

Daddy had kept to the promise he had made to himself. He went hiking with friends, had baths on several occasions with friends on the streams. He almost drowned on his first attempt when he dived into the water without any precautions.

Not long now, the long-awaited day is now. We all set out for our summer trip. We sang together, ate together, it was a long trip from QqQqQq to Salento Columbia. It was as though the weather had changed. I can feel the cool breeze. Indeed the sight was one to behold. It feels like we were being featured in the movies. I have never seen trees as tall as this, only in the movies.

The Palms looked evergreen, ever fresh, a beauty to behold. I couldn't take my eyes off it. How they rise triumphantly regardless of what was around them confident in their roots to grow as tall as they are with its peaceful nature as it bends towards the direction of the winds. No wonder the Palms symbolizes great strength, victory, and peace.

We had so much fun at the stream that cool evening, but I barely took my eyes away from the beauty of these palms and the lessons I have learned. I can't wait to share this with my friends, so I nicknamed myself as PALMS.

THE BLUE OCEAN

There are days that seem like it will never be over. Days where it seems like your entire life will end, as every activity done, takes a toll on you, from your annoying boss to some annoying customers.

This has been my daily routine. My nights are no different. My heart burns from the excessive caffeine I take to keep me on the job. Life is not as easy as I thought it would be. I had my entire life planned out with set goals and achievements to acquire. I always strive for the best, but the best never comes easy at all.

Gone are the days when you had someone do all the house chores, prepare your breakfast, and just have you wake up like a queen to the tables. Being an adult is not as easy as I thought. Now I yearn for the days before the ocean, with a cool breeze and the singing waves, the flip flop sound as dolphins delve from one point to the other. Just that sanity, where my head can clear out from all these emotional drama and affairs of life.

These thoughts ran through my head as I walk through the hospital lobby. My youngest son has been diagnosed with cancer of the lungs; we were told he had a few months to live.

Few minutes later, I was in Kanye's ward. His bed was close to the window, where he actually takes a view when he feels like. He basically spends a major part of his day doing that. Today was no different as I met him on his regular wheelchair beside this window; he was being attended to by his nurse.

Kanye is a killer for nature's gentle touch. He is either looking out the window or reading his books. They were always books that talk about nature. Kanye would always ask, Mama, why don't we have a house around an ocean? Have you ever seen a dolphin before? Why is the wind around the ocean cooler than that we have here? Do oceans ever get tired of ever-flowing? Do oceans die? Can they ever dry up?

He would always say, "I want to be like the ocean, when can I see one?"

Lost in my thoughts I heard him call "mummy."

"Your eyes are heavy" he said.

Can I be your Blue Ocean?

I looked deep into his blue eyes. It reminds me of a rhyme from a page in his book. I picked him up and lay him on his bed as he sat up straight, he rests his back on the soft and gentle pillow, picked up his book and searched for that page. He reads;

I hear you call from upon the waters; my heart skips as your voice roars as that of the waves of the ocean. I see your eyes, so blue worthy to look upon. My heavy heart race would need your gentle touch to calm.

My feet are wobbling, and my body is calling. My nights are scary, my eyes are teary and dreary. I need your touch to help calm my storm.

But when my heart rise like the ocean rise, who will calm this storm?

The gentle wind hovers as it spoke, I can't but hear peace. So I'm calm as I rest in its embrace.

As he read, I lay my head beside him as I pictured every word he said and beyond. I could see us holding hands, as Kanye ran towards the ocean just some feet away, he laughed as hard as he placed his feet on the shore. The waves came and splashed the waters on him. For once, I saw my Kanye differently, not as the dying child, but one full of life. Somehow I found peace. Indeed you are my Ocean.

Chapter Five: Other Stories

THREE SIMPLE RULES

A long time ago in Thailand, there was a wealthy man. His name was Chalong. He was a rich man. However, he needed more wealth, more cash.

One day he was strolling in his nursery. He saw an unusual fledgling in a hedge. It was little. In any case, it had wonderful and beautiful highlights. Its voice was likewise lovely. Chalong had never observed such a winged creature in his life. He gradually went close to the bramble inconspicuous. He got the bird. Now, the fledgling started to talk.

"Why have you gotten me?" the feathered creature inquired.

"I need to bring in cash. I can sell you for a major sum," answered Chalong.

"In any case, you are now rich. For what reason do you need more?" asked the winged animal.

"Since I need to get more extravagant and more extravagant," answered Chalong.

"Be that as it may, don't fantasy about bringing in cash through me!" said the feathered creature. It further included, "You can not sell me. Nobody will get me, because, in detainment, I lose my magnificence and my sweet voice." Then it gradually transformed into a dark winged creature.

The excellent highlights were currently resembling the plumes of a crow.

Chalong, any expectations of bringing in cash, were broken. He said irately, "I will slaughter you, and I will eat your meat."

"Eat me! I am so little. You won't get any meat out of me," answered the winged creature.

Chalong couldn't reply. The fledgling at that point recommended, "All around set me free. Consequently, I will show you three simple; however, helpful principles."

"What is the use of the principles? I just need cash," said Chalong. He was bothered.

"Be that as it may, these principles can benefit you incredibly," said the flying creature.

"Benefit me! Truly? At that point, I will liberate you. How might I confide in you? You may take off," said Chalong.

"I give you my word. What's more, I generally keep my words," said the flying creature.

Chalong needed to take a risk. He released the feathered creature. It flew up at once. At that point, it sat on the part of a tree. Its shading began evolving. It became wonderful once more.

Chalong asked, "Now, show me the principles."

"Unquestionably," said the winged animal.

At that point, it stated, "The main principle is Never Believe all that others state. The subsequent principle is Never tragic about something you don't have. The third principle is Never discard what you have in your grasp."

"Your senseless feathered creature," yelled Chalong. What's more, he included, "These three guidelines are known to each one. You have tricked me."

The winged animal stated, "Chalong, simply plunk down for some time. Consider every one of your activities today. You had me in your grasp, yet you released me (discharged me). You accepted all that I said. Also, you are dismal about not having me. The principles are simple. In any case, you never tailed them. Presently do you see the estimation of the guidelines?" so saying this, the winged animal took off and vanished from his sight.

THE ARROGANT SWANS

In a distant realm, there was a stream. This waterway was home to numerous brilliant swans. The swans invested the greater part of their energy in the banks of the waterway. At regular intervals, the swans would leave a brilliant plume as an expense for using the lake. The fighters of the realm would gather the plumes and store them in the regal treasury.

At some point, a destitute fowl saw the waterway. "The water right now so cool and calming. I will make my home here," thought the fledgling.

When the winged creature settled down close to the stream, the brilliant swans saw her. They came yelling. "This waterway has a place with us. We pay a brilliant quill to the King to use this stream. You can not live here."

"I am destitute, siblings. I also will pay the lease. It will be ideal if you give me cover," the fledgling argued. "By what method will you pay the lease? You don't have brilliant quills," said the swans chuckling. They further included "Quit dreaming and leave once." The unassuming winged animal argued commonly. However, the haughty swans drove the winged creature away.

"I will show them a thing or two!" said the mortified feathered creature.

She went to the King and stated, "O King! The swans in your stream are discourteous and cruel. I asked for cover, yet they said that they had bought the stream with brilliant plumes."

The King was irate with the haughty swans for having offended the destitute fowl. He requested his officers to carry the haughty swans to his court. In a matter of moments, all the brilliant swans were brought to the King's court.

"Do you think the imperial treasury relies on your brilliant plumes? You can not choose who lives by the waterway. Leave the waterway at once, or all of you will be beheaded!" yelled the King.

The swans shuddered with dread on hearing the King. They took off never to return. The feathered creature manufactured her home close to the stream and lived there cheerfully until the end of time. The winged animal offered asylum to every other fowl in the waterway.

THE IGNORANT MAN

There was a town in a realm. There was a milkman. His name was Deena. He had fabricated his cottage far away from his town, in the forested areas. He cherished the quietness of the forested areas as opposed to the uproarious air of the town. He lived in his cottage with his two dairy animals. He took care of them well and took appropriate consideration of them. Ordinarily, he took the two dairy animals to a close-by lake to shower them. The two bovines gave more milk.

Deena was a fair man. Even though he was content, on occasion, he would be fretful. "There is such a lot of off-base and evil right now. Is there nobody to direct the individuals?" this idea made him pitiful from time to time.

One night, the uninformed man, Deenu was getting back in the wake of selling milk in the town. He saw a holy person sitting under a tree and contemplating. He gradually approached him and trusted that the holy person would open his eyes. He was glad to be with the holy person for quite a while. He chose to hold up there till the holy person opened his eyes.

Sooner or later, the holy person gradually opened his eyes. He was astounded to see a man quietly sitting alongside him.

"What do you need?" asked the holy person modestly.

"I need to know what the way to Truth and Piety? Where will I discover Honesty?" asked Deena.

The holy person grinned and stated, "Go to the lake close by and ask the fish a similar inquiry. She will offer you the response."

At that point, as requested, the oblivious man, Deena went to the close-by lake and posed a similar inquiry to the fish. The fish stated, "O kind man! To start with, present to me some water to drink." Deny was astonished. He stated, "You live in water. However, you, despite everything, need water to drink? How weird!"

As of now, the fish answered, "You are correct. What's more, that offers you the response to your inquiry also. Truth, Piety, and trustworthiness are inside the core of a man. Be that as it may, being oblivious, he looks for them in the external world. Rather than meandering to a great extent, search inside yourself, and you will discover them."

This gave a tremendous fulfillment to Deena. He expressed gratitude toward the fish and strolled home a more astute man. He changed the manner by which he saw this world just like himself. From that day, Deena never felt eager.

He took his best to convey this back rub to the remainder of his kindred individuals. Every one of his companions acknowledged him as their Lord and counseled him to beat their psychological issues. He drove them appropriately.

GRACE AND LOLA

Once upon a time, there was a lord and sovereign, who had a solitary little girl. Her exceptional excellence, sweetness, and insight made her be named Grace. She was her mom's delight. Consistently she had given her an alternate dress, of gold brocade, velvet, or glossy silk; yet she was neither conceited nor bombastic. She used to spend her mornings in the study, and toward the evening, she sat sewing by the sovereign's side. She had, notwithstanding, a lot of playtime, and sweetmeats without end, so she was through and through the most joyful princess alive.

At a similar court was an old youngster named Duchess Grignon, who was the extreme opposite of Grace. Her hair was red hot red, her face fat and spotty, and she had yet one eye. Her mouth was huge to such an extent that you may have figured she could gobble you up, just she had no teeth to do it with; she was also humpbacked and faltering. Obviously, she was unable to support her grotesqueness, and nobody would have disdained her for that, if she had not been of such a disagreeable temper, that she detested everything sweet and lovely, and particularly Grace. She had an excellent assessment of herself also, and when anyone adulated the princess, would state indignantly, "That is an untruth! My little finger merits her entire body."

Over time, the sovereign fell ill and died, and her girl was nearly grieved. So was her significant other for a year, and then, he started to comfort himself by chasing. At some point, after a long pursue, he went to a weird mansion, which happened to be that of Duchess Grignon. She, educated regarding his methodology, went out to meet him and got him most consciously. As he was hot with chasing, she brought him into the coolest spot in the royal residence, which was a vaulted cavern, most exquisitely outfitted, where there were 200 barrels masterminded in long columns.

"Madam, are these all yours?" asked the ruler.

"Truly, sire, yet I will be generally cheerful if you will agree to taste our wine. Which wine do you like – canary, seclusion, champagne?" and she ran over a considerable rundown, out of which his greatness settled on his decision.

Grignon took a little mallet, and struck "toc, toc," on the barrel, from which there revealed a bunch of silver cash. "Nay, what is this?" said she, grinning, and gave to the following, from which, when she tapped it, out poured a surge of gold coins. "I never observed the like-what garbage!" and she tried the third, out of which came a stack of pearls and precious stones, so the floor of the cavern was strewn with them. "Sire," she shouted, "somebody has denied me of my great wine, and set this trash in its proper place."

"Junk, madam! Why such trash would purchase my entire realm."

"It is yours, sire," answered the duchess, "if you will make me your sovereign."

The lord, who was an incredible admirer of cash, answered energetically, "Definitely, madam, I'll wed you tomorrow, maybe."

Grignon, profoundly pleased, made yet one other condition that she ought to have Princess Grace altogether in her own standard and influence, similarly, as though she had been her genuine mother; to which the stupid ruler consented, for he figured considerably more of wealth than he did of his youngster. So he and Grognon withdrew connected at the hip out of the cavern, very much satisfied.

At the point when the lord got back, Grace ran out with bliss to respect her dad and inquired as to whether he had a great game in his chasing.

"Truly, my youngster," said he, "for I have taken a bird alive."

"Goodness, give it to me, and I will sustain and value it," cried the princess.

"That is unimaginable, for it is the Duchess Grognon, whom I have vowed to wed."

"She a pigeon – she is fairly a bird of prey," murmured the princess hopelessly; yet her dad bade her hold her tongue, and guarantee to adore her stepmother.

The loyal princess went to her condo, where her attendant before long discovered the distress on her face and its motivation.

"My youngster," said old fashioned lady, " princesses should demonstrate a good guide to humbler ladies. Allow me to put forth a valiant effort to satisfy your dad, and to make yourself pleasant to the stepmother he has decided for you. She may not be so terrible after all."

Also, the medical caretaker offered such a lot of good guidance, that Grace started to grin, and dressed herself in her best clothing, a green robe weaved with gold; while her reasonable, free-falling hair was embellished, as per the design of the day, with a coronet of jasmine, of which the leaves were made of huge emeralds.

Grignon, on her part, made the best of herself that was conceivable. She put on a high-obeyed shoe to show up less faltering, she cushioned her shoulders, colored her red hair dark, and put in a bogus eye; at that point dressed in a hooped slip of glossy violet silk cut with blue, and an upper outfit of yellow with green ribands. Now, she wished to enter the city riding a horse, as she comprehended the sovereigns were prone to do.

Meanwhile, Grace held up in dread the snapshot of her appearance, and, to take a breakaway, she went isolated into a little wood, where she cried and sobbed covertly, until out of nowhere there showed up before her a youthful page, whom she had never seen.

"Who are you?" she asked, "And when did his magnificence bring you into his administration?"

"I am in nobody's administration yet your own. I am Lola, a sovereign in my own nation, so that there is no imbalance of rank between us. I have cherished you long, and seen you frequently, for I have the pixie endowment of making myself undetectable. I may longer have concealed myself from you, yet for your present distress, wherein, be that as it may, I would like to be of both solace and help – a page but then a ruler, and your unwavering darling."

At these words, at once delicate and deferential, the princess, who had since a long time ago knew about the pixie ruler Lola, felt so glad that she dreaded Grognon no more. They talked a short time together and afterward came back to the royal residence, where the page helped her to mount her pony; on which she looked so wonderful, that all the new sovereign's qualities blurred into nothing in correlation, and none of the squires had eyes for any aside from Grace.

When Grognon saw it, "What!" she cried, "has this animal, the impudence to be preferably mounted over me! Drop, Miss, and let me try your pony; and your page, whom everybody has a favorable opinion of, offer him come and hold my harness."

Ruler Lola, who was the page, cast one look at Grace and complied; however, no sooner had the duchess mounted that the pony fled with her and hauled her over briers, stones, and mud, lastly tossed her into a profound dump. Her head was cut in a few spots, and her arm broken.

They got her in little pieces, similar to a messed up wineglass; never was there a poor lady of the hour in a more terrible predicament. However, regardless of her sufferings, her perniciousness remained. She sent for the ruler:

"This is all Grace's fault; she wished to murder me. I want that your grandness will rebuff her, or leave me to do it – else I will positively be vindicated upon you both."

The lord, scared of losing his barrels brimming with gold pieces, consented, and Grace was instructed to show up. The brutal Grognon requested four ladies, terrible as witches, to take her and strip off her fine garments, and whip her with bars till her white shoulders were red with blood. Be that as it may, lo! when the poles contacted her, they transformed into groups of plumes, and the ladies tired themselves to death with whipping, without harming Grace the least on the planet!

"Ok! kind Lola, what do I not owe you? What should I manage without you!" moaned the princess when she was reclaimed to her own chamber and her attendant. And afterward, she saw the sovereign remaining before her, in his green dress and his white crest, the most beguiling of pages.

Lola exhorted her to imagine sickness because of the coldblooded treatment she should have gotten, which so pleased Grognon, that she got well all the sooner, and the marriage was praised with extraordinary quality.

Before long, the lord, who realized that his significant other's frail point was her vanity, gave a competition, at which he requested the six most daring knights of the court to declare that Queen Grognon was the most attractive woman alive. No knight dared to debate this reality until there seemed one which conveyed a little box decorated with jewels and declared out loud that Grognon was the ugliest lady known to man, and that the most wonderful was she whose picture was in the case. He opened it, and see the picture of Princess Grace.

The princess sat behind her stepmother, felt sure that the obscure knight was Lola; however, she challenged state nothing. The challenge was fixed for the following day; however, meanwhile, Grognon, wild with outrage, instructed Grace to be taken in the night to a timberland a hundred alliances far off, brimming with wolves, lions, tigers, and bears. Futile the poor lady entreated that the orderlies would murder her at once, as opposed leave her in that appalling summit: the sovereign's requests must have complied; no answer was made to her, yet the workers remounted and rode away. Grace, in isolation and obscurity, grabbed through the timberland, sometimes falling against the trunks of trees, sometimes tearing herself with shrubs and briers; finally, defeat with dread and misery, she sank on the ground, crying out, "Lola, Lola, have you rejected me?"

While she talked, a splendid light amazed her eyes, and the 12 PM woodland was changed into sparkling rear entryways, toward the end of which seemed a royal residence of the gem, sparkling like the sun. She realized it was the doing of the pixie sovereign who adored her, and felt a delight blended with dread. She went flying, yet observed him remaining before her, more attractive and beguiling than any time in recent memory.

"Princess," said he, "for what reason would you say you fear me? This is the castle of the pixie sovereign, my mom, and the princesses my sisters, who will deal with you, and love you softly. Enter this chariot, and I will take you there."

Grace entered, and going through numerous exquisite backwoods dell, where it was clear light, and shepherds and shepherdesses were moving to cheerful music, they arrived at the castle, where the sovereign and her two girls got the pitiful princess with extraordinary generosity, and drove her through numerous rooms of rock-precious stone, sparkling with gems, where, incredibly, Grace saw the history of her own life, even down to this experience in the woods, painted on the dividers.

"How is this?" she said. "Sovereign, you know it all about me."

"Indeed, and I wish to protect everything concerning you," said he softly, after that Grace cast down her eyes. She was very much cheerful and apprehensive that she ought to figure out how to adore the pixie ruler to an extreme.

She went through eight days in his castle – days brimming with each happiness, and Lola attempted all the contentions he could consider to actuate her to wed him and stay there forever. Be that as it may, the great and delicate Grace recalled her dad, who was once so kind to her, and she favored preferably to endure over to be needing in obligation. She pestered Lola to use his pixie capacity to send her home once more, and meanwhile to mention to her what had happened to her dad.

"Accompany me into the extraordinary pinnacle, and you will see with your own eyes."

"She won't be a lot of misfortune, sire; and as, when dead, she was very horrible for you to see, I have offered requests to cover her at once."

She may well say that, for she had an enormous faggot placed in a box, and fixed up; the lord and all the country grieved over it, and now, that she was no more, they proclaimed there never was such a sweet animal as the lost princess.

Seeing her dad's misery defeated Grace. "Gracious, Lola!" she cried, "my dad thinks am dead. If you love me, take me home."

The sovereign asserted, however, tragically, saying that she was as brutal to him as Grognon was to her. As they stopped the yard, they heard an incredible clamor, and Grace saw the royal residence all self-destructing with an extraordinary accident.

"What is this?" she cried, frightened.

"Princess, my royal residence, which you neglect, is between the things which are no more, dead and gone. You will not enter it anymore till after your entombment."

"Ruler, you are furious with me," said Grace gloomily; just she knew well that she endured very as much as he did in subsequently leaving and stopping him.

Shown up in her dad's essence, she had incredible trouble in convincing him that she was not an apparition until the pine box with the faggot inside was taken up, and Grognon's perniciousness found But still, after all that, the ruler was so frail a man, that the sovereign before long caused him to accept he had been cheated, that the princess was dead, and this was a bogus Grace. Without more ado, he relinquished his girl to her stepmother's will.

Grignon moved with bliss, hauled her to a dull jail, removed her garments, made her dress in clothes, feed on bread and water, and sleep upon straw. Sad, Grace challenged not presently call upon Lola; she questioned if he despite everything adored her enough to go to her guide.

Meantime, Grognon had sent for a pixie, who was barely less pernicious than herself. "I have here," said she, "a little scalawag of a young lady for whom I wish to discover a wide range of troublesome undertakings; help me in giving her another one consistently."

The pixie vowed to consider it, and before long brought a skein as thick as four people, yet made out of string so fine, that it broke on the off chance that you just blew upon it, thus tangled that it had neither start nor end. Grignon, charmed, sent for her poor detainee.

"There, miss, show your ungainly fingers to loosen up this skein, and if you break a solitary string, I will excoriate you alive. Start when you like, yet you should complete at dusk, or it will be more regrettable for you." Then she sent her to her hopeless cell and treble-bolted the entryway.

Grace stood terrified, turning the skein again and again, and breaking several strings each time. "Ok! Lola," she cried hopelessly, "come and help me, or possibly get my last goodbye."

Promptly Lola remained close to her, having entered the cell as effectively as though he conveyed the key in his pocket. "See me, princess, prepared to serve you, even though you neglected me." He contacted the skein with his wand, and it unraveled itself and wrapped itself up in impeccable request. "Do you wish much else, madam?" asked he briskly.

"Lola, Lola, don't censure me; I am very much troubled."

"It is your own issue. Accompany me and make us both glad." But she didn't utter a word, and the pixie sovereign vanished.

At nightfall, Grognon enthusiastically went to the jail entryway with her three keys and discovered Grace grinning and reasonable, her undertaking all done. There was no grievance to make, yet Grognon shouted that the skein was messy, and boxed the princess' ears till her ruddy cheeks turned yellow and blue. At that point, she left her and overpowered the pixie with rebukes.

"find me, by to-morrow, something totally inconceivable for her to do."

The pixie brought an extraordinary bushel loaded with plumes, culled from each type of fowl – songbirds, canaries, linnets, warblers, pigeons, thrushes, peacocks, ostrich, birds, partridges, jaybirds, falcons – indeed, if I revealed to them all finished, I will never reach a conclusion; and every one of these quills was so mixed up, that they couldn't be recognized.

"See," said the pixie, "even one of ourselves would think that its hard to isolate these, and mastermind them as having a place with each kind of fledgling. Order your detainee to do it; she makes certain to come up short."

Grignon bounced for satisfaction, sent for the princess, and requested her to take her errand, and finish it, as in the past, by sunset.

Grace attempted calmly. However, she could see no distinction in the plumes; she tossed them all back again into the container and started to sob harshly. "Allow me to pass on," she said, "for death just will end mine distresses. Lola adores me never again; if he did, he would as of now have been here.

"My princess, I'm here," cried a voice from under the bushel; and the pixie sovereign showed up. He gave the 3 taps with his wand – the plumes flew by millions out of the bushel, and engineered themselves in little loads, each having a place with an alternate feathered creature.

"how do I repay you?" cried Grace.

"Love me!" addressed the ruler, gently, and said no more.

When Grognon showed up, she found the errand done. She was angry at the pixie, who was a lot more surprised herself at the result of their noxious inventions. However, she vowed to try once more. For a few days, using all her industry in concocting a crate, which, she stated, the detainee won't be able to open. "At that point," included the guile pixie, "obviously, being such an insubordinate and fiendish young lady, as you state, she will open it, and the outcome will fulfill you however much you might want."

Grignon took the case, and told Grace to convey it to her château, and set it on a specific table, in a loft she named, yet not upon any record, to open it or inspect its substance.

Grace withdrew. She was dressed like any poor laborer, in a cotton outfit, a woolen hood and wooden shoes; yet, as she strolled along, individuals took her for a sovereign in camouflage, so beautiful were her looks and ways. In any case, being frail with detainment, she before long became tired, and, plunking downward on the edge of a little wood, took the crate upon her lap, out of nowhere a outstanding want held onto her to open it.

"I will take nothing out, I will contact nothing," said she to herself, "yet I should perceive what is inside."

Without thinking about the outcomes, she lifted up the top. She quickly there leaped out various little men and little ladies, conveying little tables and seats, little dishes, and minimal instruments. The entire organization was little to such an extent that the greatest monster among them was hardly the stature of a finger. They jumped into the green knoll, isolated into different groups, and started moving and singing, eating and drinking, to Grace's marvel and joy. Yet, when she recalled herself and wished to get them into the crate once more, they all rushed away, played at finding the stowaway in the wood, and in no way, shape or form would she be able to get a single one.

Once more, in her trouble, she called upon Lola, and again he showed up; and, with a single pinch of his wand, sent all the little individuals once more into the container. At that point, in his chariot, drawn by stags, he took her to the mansion, where she did all that she had been told, and returned in wellbeing, to her stepmother, who was angrier than ever in recent memory. If a pixie could be choked, Grognon unquestionably would have done it in her fury. Finally, she made plans to ask help no more, yet to work her own devious will upon Grace.

She caused to dive an enormous gap in the nursery, and taking the princess there, indicated her the stone which secured it.

"Underneath this stone lies an incredible fortune; lift it up, and you will see."

Grace complied, and keeping in mind that she was remaining at the edge of the pit. After this, there appeared to be no more trust in the poor princess.

"O Lola," cried she, "you are retaliated for. For what reason did I not return your adoration, and wed you! Passing will be less severe if just you lament me a bit."

While she talked, she saw through the clear murkiness a gleam of light; it got through a little entryway. She recollected what Lola had stated: that she could stay away forever to the pixie royal residence, until after she was covered. Maybe this last remorselessness of Grognon would be the end of her distresses. So she took mental fortitude, crawled through the little entryway, and lo! she turned out into an excellent nursery, with extended rear entryways, natural product trees, and blossom beds. Well, she knew it, and well, she knew the sparkle of the stone precious stone dividers. Also, there, at the royal residence entryway, stood Lola, and the sovereign, his mom, and the princesses, his sisters. "Welcome, Grace!" cried they all, and Grace, after the entirety of her sufferings, sobbed for euphoria.

The marriage was commended with extraordinary wonder, and all the pixies, for a thousand classes round, went to it. Some came in chariots drawn by mythical serpents, or swans, or peacocks; some were mounted upon drifting mists or globes of fire. Among the rest, showed up the very pixie who had helped Grognon to torment Grace. At the point when she found that Grognon's poor detainee was currently Prince Lola's lady of the hour, she was overpowered with disarray and begged her to overlook all that had passed, in light of the fact that she truly was oblivious who she had been so pitilessly harrowing.

"However, I will present appropriate reparations in light of all the evil that I have done," said the pixie; and, declining to remain for the wedding-supper, she remounted her chariot, drawn by two horrible snakes, and travelled to the royal residence of Grace's dad. There, under the steady gaze of either lord, or squires, or women in-waiting could stop her – she came behind the insidious Grognon, and turned her neck, similarly as a cook does a horse shelter entryway fowl. So Grognon died and was covered, and nobody was especially upset for the equivalent.

THE CLEVER EUNICE

There was a man who had a girl, who was classified "Smart Eunice," and when she was grown up, her dad stated, "We should see about her wedding."

"Truly," answered her mom, "at any point, a youngster will show up who is deserving of her."

Finally, a specific youth, by the name Hans, originated from separation to make a proposition of marriage; however, he required one condition, that the Clever Eunice ought to be extremely reasonable.

"Goodness," said her dad, "no dread of that! she has a head loaded with cerebrums;" and the mother included, "Ah, she can see the breeze explode the road, and hear the flies hack!"

"Great," answered Hans; "however, recall, if she isn't exceptionally wise, I won't take her." Soon, they plunked down to supper, and her mom stated, "Eunice, go down into the basement and draw some lager."

So Clever Eunice brought the container down from the divider, and went into the basement, jolting the top here and there on her way, to take a break. When she got the first floor, she drew a stool and set it before the container, all together that she probably won't need to stop, for she figured stooping may harm her back, and give it an unwanted twist. Then she put the can before her and turned the tap, and keeping in mind that the brew was running, as she didn't want her eyes to be inactive, she looked about upon the divider above and underneath. Then she saw, after much peeping into every corner, an axe, which the bricklayers had abandoned, standing out of the roof directly over her head. At seeing this Clever Eunice started to cry, saying, "Goodness! in the event that I wed Hans, and we have a kid, and he grows up, and we send him into the basement to draw brew, the axe will fall upon his head and murder him;" thus she stayed there sobbing energetically over the looming hardship.

In the end, the great people upstairs were sitting tight for the lager. However as Clever Eunice didn't come, her mom advised the house cleaner to take a quick trip and see what she was halting for. The house cleaner went down into the basement and discovered Eunice sitting before the container crying healthily, and she asked, "Eunice, what are you sobbing about?"

"Ok," she answered, "have I not cause? If I wed Hans, and we have a youngster, and he grows up, and we send him an errand here to draw lager, that ax will fall upon his head and execute him."

"Gracious," said the house cleaner, "what a cunning Eunice we have!" And, plunking down, she started to sob, as well, for the adversity that was to occur.

Inevitably, when the worker didn't return, many people above started to feel parched, so the spouse advised the kid to go down into the basement and see what had happened to Eunice and the housekeeper. The kid went down, and there sat Clever Eunice and the house cleaner both crying, so he asked what happened; and Eunice revealed to him a similar story, of the ax that was to fall on her youngster, if she wedded Hans, and if they had a kid. When she had completed, the kid shouted, "What a sharp Eunice we have!" and fell sobbing and wailing with the others.

Upstairs they were all the while waiting, and the spouse stated, when the kid didn't return, "Do you go down, wife, into the basement and see why Eunice remains so long." So she went down and discovering every one of the three stayings there crying, asked for an explanation, and Eunice educated her regarding the ax, which should definitely fall upon the head of her child. At that point, the mother in like manner shouted, "Gracious, what a wise Eunice we have!" and, plunking down, started to sob as much as any of the rest.

In the end, the spouse waited for his significant other's arrival; however, finally, he felt so parched, that he stated, "I should go myself down into the basement and see what is keeping our Eunice." As soon as he entered the basement, where he found the four sitting and crying together, and when he heard the explanation, he also shouted, "Goodness, what a clever Eunice we have!" and plunked down to cry with the whole of his lungs.

This time the groom above sat, waiting, yet when nobody returned, he figured they should be waiting for him. Thus he went down to perceive what was wrong. At the point when he entered, there sat the five crying and moaning, everyone louder than his neighbor.

"What adversity has occurred?" he inquired.

"Ok, dear Hans!" cried Eunice, "if you and I wed each other, and have a kid, and he grow up, and we, maybe, send him down to this basement to tap the lager, the ax which has been left standing up there may fall on his head, thus slaughter him: and do you not think this is sufficient to sob about?"

"Now," said Hans, "more judiciousness than this isn't essential for my housekeeping; since you are such a smart Eunice, I will have you for my better half." And, grasping her hand, he drove her home and commended the wedding legitimately.

After they had been married a short time, Hans said one morning, "Spouse, I will go out to work and win some cash; go into the field and assemble some corn wherewith to make bread."

As she went to the field, she said to herself, "What will I do? Will, I cut first, or eat first? Ay, I will eat first!" Then she gobbled up the substance of her pot. When it was done, she contemplated internally, "now, will I procure first or sleep first? I figure I will have a snooze!" thus, she laid herself down among the corn, and rested.

In the end, Hans got back, yet Eunice didn't come. Thus he stated, "Goodness, what a reasonable Eunice I have! She is innovative to the point that she doesn't get back home to eat anything." Then, the evening came, and still, she didn't return; so Hans went out to see the amount she had harvested; in any case, see, nothing by any means, and there lay Eunice sleeping soundly among the corn! So home, he ran quickly and brought a net with little ringers holding tight it, which he tossed over her head while she, despite everything rested on. When he had done this, he returned again and closed to the house-entryway, and, seating himself on his stool, started working enterprisingly.

Finally, when it was about to dim, the Clever Eunice got up, and when she stood up, the net fell all over her hair, and the chimes jingled at each progression she took. This startled her, and she started to question whether she was an extremely Clever Eunice, and said to herself, "Am I she, or am I not?" This was an inquiry she was unable to reply, and she stopped for a drawn-out period of time considering about it. Finally, she figured she would return home and ask whether she was truly herself, assuming somebody would have the option to advise her. At the point when she went to the house-entryway, it was closed, so she tapped at the window, and asked, "Hans, is Eunice inside?" "Yes," he answered, "she is." At which answer she turned out to be truly startled, and shouting, "Ah, paradise, at that point, I am not Eunice!" she approached another house, expecting to pose a similar inquiry. Be that as it may, when the people inside heard the jingling of the ringers in her net, they wouldn't open their entryways, and nobody would get her. So she fled from the town, and nobody has ever seen her since.

Chapter 6:
Stories of the Countryside

<u>DOG</u>

JOSH AND BUDDY, THE FLUPPY PUPPY

Once upon a time, in the country-side suburb lived a young lad, Josh, and his family, which dwelt in their farm-yard. Josh is a boisterous young lad, fair as the sun with blackheads running riots on his face. He wore a yellow curly hair; he was fond of two things in the entire world, his father and pets that were gifted to him by his father. Josh was the first of three; he was popularly called, Josh!!The farm-boy by his peers, this is irrespective of the fact that farming and ranching was a popular enterprise in this settlement his family abodes. Josh seemed emotionally drifted since he lost his dad to an ailment. Josh and his family had since struggled to meet up with the financial quota for the family.

Josh, as every lad of his cadre, always fancied playing with his peers in the fields from mid-afternoon to the evening. As opposed to the parents of his friends, Josh's mom is skeptical about staying out late, and she always warns Josh to make haste to be home before 6'O clock. Josh heeled briskly through the Allen's walk-way en-route his home this very evening. He hast to meet up with curfew this very evening, as he ran through the sand path, his heart raced, and he felt different. Maybe what troubled his mind was how to avoid the constant nagging from his mom. Suddenly he heard a noise from the waste-bins that lay across the path, and he flipped in agitation. He literally skipped a beat; he then halted and walked in stealth fashion. As he drew near, as it was for an exploring lad of such caliber. He beckoned and raised the cans, to his amazement lay a white-furred puppy covered in patched mud. The eyes of this puppy were dark and alluring, and the mild cry aroused pity in the heart of Josh. Compassion filled the heart of Josh, and he picked up the puppy and placed it between its arms. Thoughts raced through his mind, I am definitely keeping this one, whether his mom was going to nag or spank him did not bother him. Since his dad's demise, she suggested he let go of their flamboyant lifestyle and opts for a decent lifestyle. He had to grudging let go of his pet, Nemo the gold-fish and Frankie the Wistar mice.

Josh strolled in gentle strides along the sandy foot-walk with green stout grass at both sides. He pelted the furs of the puppy as he walked and thought of names for his new pet flew across his mind. He said to himself, I should name him Jack, No!! Jack is quite a common name for puppies. I should name him buddy, buddy is nice, he said to himself. He hopped joyfully as he headed home, buddy, my buddy!! He said.

On arrival, Josh snuck to his room and prepared a warm bath and washed off the mud from the body of buddy. Josh, in a long while, seem filled with joy, he raced to show his mom his new friend. Josh's mom, Alexis, was at the dining table, set for supper. Josh raced to din from his room with Buddy, in his arm, and said to his mom, " mom look who I found," his name is buddy. Alexis was furious, as Josh was expected to have arrived earlier to assist prepare for dinner, she replied in harshest of words, "Josh would you return that creature from where you picked it from, we have more mouths to feed than hands to work". She continued, "you have chosen not to come to terms with reality, stupid child." Josh was crushed to the bones, he always wondered if Alexis was his biological mom. He fled to the farm-yard in resentment.

Josh usually found solace at the porch in the farmyard; he sat there staring to the moon, and his hands were found pelting the furs of buddy. He wondered why his mom complained a lot and why his father had to abandon him and his siblings on earth so early. Josh always felt abandoned and lonely, but on the bright-side maybe Buddy was God-sent to be his company, finally God heard his prayers, he figured. He made that brighten grimace. He refused to eat, but he felt warm because of his newfound company. Josh and buddy slept in the farm-yard that night.

Josh's farm-house was built as a scattered settlement was surrounded by tall trees and bushes, as the trade was farming. Trades also ride along with their hazards. They are like Siamese twins. The local council has put out a warning to locals to deceased from uncontrolled bush burning as it put lives at risk. Many of the locals tend to carry out their evil menace in the dead of night. Unfortunately, that night, a certain farmer indulged in bush burning, and the fire drifted out of control. The fire burned fiercely, and burning down everything and anything that stood its way, it burnt it down into ashes.

The bush continued to burn hesitantly, but as folks would say, sometimes, blessings come in disguise. Buddy woke up and began to bark unceasingly woo!! Woo!! Josh said in a sleepy tone, sleep buddy, you are making a lot of noise. Josh's words seem to be fuel to fire, and Buddy kept on barking. Josh, in annoyance, reluctantly woke up. As Josh stood up from where he laid, he perceived fumes of smoke, he wondered to himself, "who would be cooking at the early hours of the morning." But the fumes seem enormous to be from cooking. Josh and buddy hurried out of the farm-house to investigate, and to his amazement, he saw climbing soot to the clouds, and blazing fire raged through like a horde of horses. Josh immediately, he took to his heels, yelling, "Mom!! Mom!! Wake up, Fire!! Fire!! Alexis woke up like someone experiencing a nightmare. She heeled out and found the same scary sights. Josh headed to his sibling's room and woke them up. The down-size of where Josh resided was that houses were far apart. You would have to walk meters to get to your neighbor. Alexis took her children, the livestock they would gather and buddy and fled for safety. As they walked, Josh recounted the ordeal, and all that Alexis thought was that, "the one thing she feared has befell them" But certainly, buddy is not just a member of the family but he saved their lives today.

The End.

FLOWERS

THE PURPLE ALOE

Once upon a time, in a far-away country lived a rich merchant and his family. The merchant had all he desired as pertaining to material acquisitions, but he would bear a seed. Life can be ironical, he wondered. He sought the advice of many wise folks and drank different potions to enable his wife to conceive but all to no avail. One faithful day, he was returning from one of his numerous trading sojourns in his cart. As they rode speedily, he gazed through the window of his cart as he drowned in his own thoughts. Suddenly, he saw an old man, half-naked with bruises and sores plaguing his entire body. He looked like someone who was a victim of snares of the night, which would be referred to as the claws of robbers. The rich merchant was hesitant to highlight as he thought that it would be a trap, but on taking a second consideration on the matter, he signaled his cart-rider to halt. The rich merchant stepped out and approached the old man. The old man narrated his ordeal, how he was ambushed by a band of thieves, and all his belongings and money were carted away. The rich merchant took the old man and headed to an inn where they passed the night. The rich man ensured that the sores and injuries of the old man were tended for, and ointments for healing were administered.

On the departure of the rich merchant, he gifted the old man some pieces of silver as financial assistance. The old man called the rich merchant and thanked him, and in gratitude, gave him seeds of flower called the purple aloe. The old man told him that it was passed unto him by his father, and the fluid that flows out of its nectar is known for its magical and fertility potency. They hugged tightly and bade themselves goodbye. The rich merchant rejoiced as he hurried home, he kept saying to himself, "the gods have found favor in my sight." On arrival home, he narrated journey tale to his wife, and she rejoiced.

That week, the rich merchant, erected a glasshouse and planted the purple aloe only. The rich merchant and his wife took conscious efforts to make a child as they drank of the potion from the purple aloe regularly. Shortly after, the wife of the rich merchant conceived a child and gave birth to a beautiful girl. The rich merchant named her flower because her birth was miraculously from the potion that runs in the veins of the purple aloe.

Flower was a beauty to behold. As she grew with every increasing inch, her fairness was like that of the sun. Her beauty was insurmountable in comparison with her peers. Her hair was long and white, falling gently off her shoulders. Before she reached the age of marriage, suitors flocked the gates of the rich merchant. These recent happening was a thing of concern for the rich merchant, his daughter was precious to him and didn't wish any harm should beset her as a result of a wrong spouse. Sometimes the rich merchant wondered if his affection for his daughter must be birth out of their long wait for her conception, fifteen long years.

When flower was of age, her father, the rich merchant, took her for a stroll around their castle. He took time to explain how much she meant to him and how her mother and him had to wait for fifteen years to conceive her. The rich merchant also told flower about the importance of the purple aloe to their family.

Men from far away countries and countries near trooped in numbers for the hand in marriage of the rich merchant's daughter, Flower. They were men of different sizes, caliber: some were sons of war-lords, princes of kingdoms and even men known for their resounding wisdom made appearance in the bit to make a bride and wife from Flower. Every suitor had their sessions with Flower, they had their opportunities to woo, some came in wearing the regalia of the wealth of their father, some came with promises that Flower would not lift a finger to carry out a core in her life. Flower was a child groomed in wisdom and seemed to be indifferent about these promises as they emanated from the mouth of a spoilt brat.

But to her amazement, there was young prince Williams who seemed different. He was tall and handsome with a charming aura. She had a lengthy conversation, and he was thoughtful to really make efforts to know her, what she likes, and her ideals. They both began to have regular walks where they talked, chatted, and laughed. She grew so fond of Williams as grew from the skin of their parent's riches to genuine relationship of simple girl meets a young boy, and they both fell in love. Just one thing seems to fall-out for Flower, concerning Williams that his country was always at war against a rival country and the kings are always short-lived as the hazard of the battles they engaged in regularly. In the case of Williams, his father and grandfather's reign was short-lived. Flower feared this gravely.

Shortly after Flower grew fond of Williams, war between his country and their rivals became eminent. She was gravely scared, but like her father told her that since her birth, their heritage seemed to be tied to the purple aloe. Before Williams headed for battle, she prepared the potion and was put into a bottle and handed it over to him. She cried and kiss him goodbye, but Williams promised Flower that he was coming back for her.

With his army, he rode into battle, and days drifted into weeks and weeks into months. With every passing day, the chances Williams was returning from the battle diminished, but Flower kept on praying relentlessly every day. This very cold evening, as Flower prayed in the purple aloe glasshouse, then she heard the whining of a galloping horse and a fair young man rode it and behold to her greatest surprise, it was Williams, her heart leaped for joy. They hugged each other tightly, and Williams recounted the stories of their victory in battle and how the potency of the purple aloe was indeed a magical and lifesaving potion. Finally, Flower and Williams got married and lived happily ever after.

The End.

DUCKS

ZACH, THE FOGGILY DUCK

Once upon a time, Papa Gander and Mama Goose were expecting their first set of off-springs. It is basically a thing of great joy for the new couple. As the culture, Gander accompanied his wife, Goose, for the routine ante-natal checks at the ducks and duckling general hospital. During the last check-up, the Doctor duck examined Goose. He noticed a discrepancy during the ultra-sound. Doctor duck made his observations know to the couples immediately. He invited the couples to his office and he said to them, "good morning," during the ultra-sound, I noticed an anomaly likely to affect one of your fetus but this usual occurrence in multiple pregnancies. Goose exclaimed in a sad tone, oh God!! What can be done to redeem this scenario, Doc, she said as her husband wrapped his arms around her in an attempt to console her? Doc responded, nodding his head in negation, "I am sorry, we cannot really do much than believe the best of outcomes." The couple left the hospital sad but kept their torch of hope burning irrespective of the news they received that morning.

Shortly after, just a few months, Goose was due for delivery, with the build-up of bouts of labor contraction that evening just a few minutes past six; she yelled her husband pet name incessantly, Hun!! I am having contractions. He immediately rushed to her aid, packed all that was required for delivery, and they headed for the hospital. Just a few minutes past eleven that night, she was delivered of five ducklings. Two ducklings were of female gender and the last three of male gender. But of the male gender, one seem special and different. He was an albino-white breed (he had no black patches), and his feet were not properly webbed, unlike his siblings who had black spots or patches littered across their white skin with normal webbed feet. He was quite small but cute and beautiful in his own way, Mama Goose called him Zach.

Zach was indeed different; he was more like a white square amongst a lot of black squares. He was spotted among the horde for his uniqueness. His peers and his siblings referred to Zach as a freak or a weirdo. Hence they nicknamed him, albino Zach, or foggily duck, and he always raced to his mum who consoled and kept ringing this words to his eardrums, "Zach my boy, you are a special one." Zach sometimes felt some truth in the words of his Mama Goose, as he has a very sensitive nostril, he would trail a duck from miles away as his nostrils pick duck scents. Zach was slow-paced, more like he did things at his own pace, he was last to swim amongst his siblings, made his first utterance (by that I mean the quack!!Quack!! Vocals) last in relation to his peers plus his distinct body features and the fact that he barely was able to make friends.

This year seems different in duck town, the month which the rain was expected to begin to grace the dry and patchy lands was far gone yet no single drop descended from the heavens. As every day passed, it seems imminent that famine was upon duck town. The famine came without any prior notification, the river began to dry up, food barns gradually emptied, and the death toll of ducks was on the rise due to diseases associated with poor nutrition and food shortage. Town meetings were called to ascertain the right step to make to curtail this disaster that has befallen duck town. The gods were consulted, but no answer or solution was obtained. Emissaries were sent out by the town council, but none returned. Most families had lost hope and prepared for the worst possible outcome, which was death.

Zach was always accustomed to always being alone, always found solace in his long and aimless strolls. As Zach strolled through a foot-path in the woods this faithful afternoon as he wondered on what has befallen his town, he perceived an unfamiliar duck scent. He was initially reluctant, yet he followed the trail, and with every step, the scent seems stronger. Somewhere in his mind, he reasoned that it was surely the emissary en-route back to duck town, finally a solution was feasible, he thought. As she got much closer, he was taken his aback by the sight, a gorgeous duck singing melodiously. From the prints on her feathers, she was obviously of a different tribe.

Zach was quite shy; he had never had a proper conversation with female counter-part. He wondered what he would say, or how he was going to introduce himself. He pondered for a while, after which he braced himself to trust his gut despite his assurance that his goofy personality might betray him.

Zach walked up to her and taps her, sorry!! He said, hello dear and he introduces himself, and he asked why she was found in the woods alone. She told him that this was her spot of solitude and that it was a regular habit of hers and in-turn she introduced her, my name is Sally, it turns out that her father was a chief of a town called Gander and Goose harbor. They both got chatty, and Zach explained the challenges that Duck town was experiencing and how they sought different option, but no positive result seem forthcoming. Sally felt sorry for Zach and promised him that she would be of assistance as it turns out that famine was just regional after-all and not global.

Zach fled home with the good news, when got to duck town, he relayed his findings to the council of chiefs. It was no news that they were going to doubt Zach, but he mightily convinced them, and they were clueless, any suggestion was an option to be explored. Some chiefs and emissaries set out for Gander and Goose harbor for answers to their woes. To their great amazement, they found Gander and Goose harbor, and all Zach said was indeed true. The folks of harbor were entertaining and warm; the chiefs of duck town were able to strike a fair deal that would ensure that the food in abundance was made available for their people. Zach was special after all, his art of adventure and uniqueness saved duck town.

The End.

The Story of Forte The Cat.

This is a story of Forte the Cat. It's Forte's first day in school, and Forte felt very uneasy, as his mum woke him up. Forte tried to lift up his closing eyelids with all the strength he could muster, he stood up, stretched and yawned before he finally looked at his mum.

"Cats are hardworking, despite being slow and lovely," said his mum. "This is six A.M Forte. It's time to wake up.

"But mum, I still want to sleep some more, I took milk and cheese in the night, and I am still giddy mum will you allow me for thirty more minutes?"

His mum went to the bathroom, brought his towel and soap, and flung at him. "As I said, Forte, it's time to wake up" other cats are already on their way to Winsophia, the Cat school. Please get up and freshen up, and we will be on our way".

Forte slowly got up from the bed, picking up his towel and soap and swaggered to the bathroom, his body slowing this way and that.

When he popped out of the bathroom, his mum had already prepared carrots and juice for breakfast, he ate, and soon enough, they were on their way to school.

It was Forte's first day in school, and he felt so uneasy, he wasn't accustomed to the classroom.

He missed home, where he would be playing with his friends Rob and Wilson and chasing rats and basking in the river.

Now he was here, so slow and lethargic, but he was determined to make something out of school, he needed to make his mum proud and be bright like his mates in school, how was Forte planning to do this? Forte decided he will pay attention in class and make friends with the most intelligent cats in class. His mother complained this morning about his laziness, he didn't like that, and he vowed not to continue like that.

Kathy appeared in front of the class, she started with "cats are nice and are lovely, this is the best cat school in Creston, and you cats here must count yourselves privileged, because many cats will want to be here but cannot because they are less privileged. So you need to make the most of this opportunity cats". "Yes, aunty Kathy" the cats echoed, and their voices reverberated in the room.

Forte was mute, he was ruminating on aunty Kathy's words, allowing each sentence to sift into his ears and Bones and marrows, passing into his soul and finding roots in his heart. He kept those words in his heart, and he was going to make the best of the opportunity in school.

He sat near Fred, a shrewd and gentle cat with nice and fresh furs, Fred was keen for knowledge. Throughout the day, Fred paid attention in class and answered questions in class. Milk and chocolates during break, and throughout this time, Forte watched him with keen interest. Fort was determined to be friends with Fred, he was convinced that friendship with Fred was going to be a very fruitful one and one that would help fuel his ambition in school, and he will make his mum proud, and aunty Kathy would be happy with him.

The bell for dismissal rang, and Fred was tidying his box when Forte appeared beside him with a bright smile. "You are a wonderful cat, Fred, and I want to be your friend, hope you don't mind." "Not at all," Fred said, making forward and kissing Forte, Forte was delighted.

And they turned and began to walk home, as they walked they talked about aunty Kathy, about winsophia, about what their parents expect from them in school. About how they would leave up to fulfilling this demands.

Fred said his mum promised to buy him a bicycle and a box of chocolates and cakes if he does well. While Forte retorted that his mum has made no promises but that he would love to make his mum proud, and he was going to do it at all costs.

They kissed each other and vowed to live to their dreams no matter what happened.

When Forte got home, his mum hugged him. "Mum school was very good today, I am getting inspired, and I will try to make the most of my time at Winsophia" his mum was so happy to hear this." Did you make any friends?" "Yes!" Forte screamed triumphantly, his lungs reverberating under his throat.

His mum reached out and hugged him so passionately, gently touching his furs, Forte was smiling, and that reassured him of his stance. Tomorrow, he will tell Fred to introduce him to other bright students in class, and he will keep on paying attention in school and pleasing his mum.

The next day in school was sports day, and the cats were all dressed in their sports wears, they were all out in the field and waited for aunty Kathy to give them instructions on how the sports day would go. Forte was with Fred at the rear of the school field.

"I would love to make more friends with the other bright students like you in class Fred," Forte said, his eyes dimming and revealing the depth of the graveness of what he said.

"It's alright, Forte, but you must know that no one was made bright. We are just a group of cats who told ourselves we were smart, and we started working as though we were, and we became that way." Forte's face tightened to a grimace, he was shocked at the words of Fred, " but my mum says, I am lazy, and I sleep too much." " That's because you think you do, and so you always catch yourself sleeping because you really think so" Forte's face lit up, and he was momentarily too stunned to speak as the reality of Fred's words, dawned on him. "Okay, how Fred, I am smart," he shouted. "That's it," Fred screamed and hugged him."

As they went home that day, Forte was so ecstatic, he had found a new light, "it doesn't take so much to be amazing after all" Forte muttered to himself under his breath. " I am a smart cat, I am so amazing."

He was so happy and was willing to share this new light with his mum.

Her face tore into a wide smile when Forte told him how smart he was, she hugged her kit and licked her furs. Forte was becoming a cat, a fantastic cat.

This is the end of the story of Forte the cat.

The Story of The Great Iroko Tree

In the hills of Normandy, there was once a selfish Iroko tree. It was so big and so luscious, it's leaves sparkled and danced. Its bark was fresh and kinky. Its root, strong and stern. But the Iroko tree lived in solitude, it made sure it's leaves dried up before it fell, it didn't provide its fruit for the animals nor did it provide shades for other trees and shrubs and animals.

Virtually, every living and non-living thing in the hills of Normandy was sore at this tree.

Its gigantic nature didn't offer anything to them, and they had pleaded severally with mother Earth to take him away. But mother Earth kept asking them one question, "what have you done for the big Iroko"? So each time the animals come to plead with mother Earth to kill off the Iroko, they all went home sullen and angry with mother Earth.

They all knew they couldn't do anything to the big Iroko, because one branch of the big Iroko would wipe out all of them. So they all resorted to sulking, they always gathered together to insult and ridicule the Iroko, but all that didn't change anything.

They keep making several plans weaving and weaving and looking for ways to take down the big Iroko.

One day, they planned to set the Iroko on fire. As they were about to carry this out when the king of rats came pleading that the sort of fire that will destroy the Iroko will also burn it's kind and that their children will die. When the other animals thought about this, they decided against the plan and didn't set the Iroko on fire.

The Iroko continued to live In its solitude, rendering no one any helps and getting no helps from anyone, and the animals kept on sulking, each time they stare at the great Iroko tree, a monsoon of bitterness welled up within them. And so, on another day, they came up with the plan to cut the tree.

But they can't get anywhere near the great Iroko, it would use it's branches and destroy all of them and so that was going to be a futile journey.

However, the fox suggested that they can make use of a hook. The plan was nice, so they planned to plant a hook on the big Iroko tree in the night while it slept and attach a very long rope, with which they will pull it down in the morning.

Three nights had passed, and they were done with the plans of hooking the great Iroko tree, they had the hook and the rope. But argued fruitlessly about who will hook the great Iroko tree.

The tortoise suggested that the lions were brave, and this was a matter that required bravery, so the Lions should not have any problems hooking the Iroko tree.

The lions complained that the noise they make would wake up the Iroko, and their plans would crumble.

The other animals reasoned that it was true, and the elephant was asked to walk slowly and attach the hook, but the elephant deferred, saying that it was difficult to do that, because they won't be swift with it.

Every animal kept on coming up with one reason or the other why they can't hook the great Iroko tree until the bull volunteered to do that.

He did that on one condition that the animals would take care of his children if he didn't survive the escapade and the other animals agreed.

So on that faithful night, the bull walked briskly, tiptoeing to where the Iroko tree was situated, it was midnight. So the Iroko tree was deep in sleep. The bull was fearless and so didn't want to make mistakes, so he rounded the Iroko tree seven times, wrapping the great Iroko tree with a rope before finally planting the hook at the bark of the stem of the Iroko tree. As soon as the hook penetrated the Iroko tree, it roused and it's branches came alive, whirling around in a circle very fiercely, and as the bull made to run away, one of the rear branches bent over and swept it off its foot, and it landed with its horn and the horn bent, as it struggled to limp away before the branch makes a fatal move on it. And so the bull escaped by a hair breadth. And the great Iroko tree struggled in futility to set itself free, but the hook remained steadfast on it. And when it found it couldn't do much about unhooking itself, it rested.

In the morning all the animals ate well and were strong and ready to pull down the great Iroko tree, they lined up on a straight file and pulled and pulled, but the Iroko tree stood strong, rooted to its spot. All the veins in all the animals were out as they pulled with all their strength, but they were all sprawling on the grass as the Iroko tree remained unmoved. They all went home, grumbling and sulking at their failed efforts.

While the earth, they complained to mother Earth, asking her why she held the root of the great iroko tree so strongly, but mother Earth greeted their complaints with derisive laughter, they were all pained, and each one went to their houses despondent.

One day, it was very cold and dry, and the leaves of the iroko tree were dry, it was so cold, and the great iroko tree was dying. The animal kingdom felt like heaven on Earth as they watched keenly waiting for when the great iroko tree would drop dead. As they watched on delight, a fair, beautiful girl emerged and looked with pity at the great iroko tree, and so she decided to protect the iroko tree, she used her big blanket to cover the great iroko tree. And the great Iroko tree survived.

The next day was sunny and hot, and the great Iroko was lush and green. It shielded the young Fair Lady from the sun, it bent over and covered her. And mother Earth called all the other animals and when they saw it, they didn't believe what they saw, and mother Earth told them that the great Iroko tree has discovered that it cannot survive on its own. And encouraged them to go and find shield under it's shadow, and they went. The Iroko tree was happy to offer then shield, and they were happy to be shielded. They all lived happily ever after.

The Grass Story

This is a bedtime story that captures the adventures of the elephant grass, spear grass, and carpet grass.

The Elephant grass, Spear grass, and Carpet grass once lived together in the hills of Bentis, and they were discontent with their place of abode, in Bentis, because they didn't like how the place looked.

"We are all alone in this place, and it's so lonely and serene, we can't even play with other plants, I hate this place so much" the Elephant grass fussed, and the Spear grass would normally nod in agreement to whatever the elephant grass said.

But the carpet grass would look at them and smile "you should be thankful for what you have, some other grasses wish to exist, but they no longer do because of one tragedy or the other. But you are still alive, you have water, and you can absorb it, the sun shines on you daily, the wind isn't very cruel to you, you basically have everything you need, so why do you whine and fuss about being lonely?"

Whenever the carpet grass stopped speaking, the elephant grass would look at it with horror and derision, and the Spear grass would also move away from the carpet grass.

They both treated the carpet grass with cruelty because the carpet grass believes that one should be content with what one has, and the elephant grass and spear grass always kept wanting more out of life.

So the Elephant grass and spear grass continued to nurse their hefty dreams, and the carpet grass, lowly and timid, was happy in its little space. It wished for somewhere better, somewhere it would have so many beautiful children, and its owners will take care of it, and its children. However, even as it craved for all this, it was content.

On the other hand, the Elephant grass and spear grass craved earnestly for the worldly pomp and power, they dreamt of being set up in a great hill, where many other plants will surround and respect them.

One day, a couple walked along the hills of Bentis, pushing their trolley and looking around to harvest species of grasses.

They dressed brightly colored cloths, the woman wore a golden earring and bangles, and the man wore a golden wristwatch and shoes.

The elephant grass drew closer to them bending over to get a better look, Its eyes lit up, it was engrossed in the grandiosity of the couple, this was what it had been hoping to get all its life.

And when the spear grass made to get closer, the Elephant grass kicked it away and remained steadfastly and conspicuously positioned, waiting earnestly for the couple to come and get it.

And when the couple finally arrived where the elephant grass was, it leaped for joy and swung itself into their trolley as the woman uprooted and made to cast it into the trolley.

They carted it way, and it danced and bounced along joyfully inside the trolley as the couple rode along.

Soon enough, the butterfly brought the news of the fate of the elephant grass to the spear grass and the carpet grass.

"The elephant grass, was planted in the valleys of kush and it was pruned and made to multiply in abundance, however when it began to multiply, the couple sent their cows to eat up all the elephant grass. And the cows are now eating all the elephant grass and defecating on all its children. The elephant grass cries all day and all night. It murmurs daily, and it agrees that the hills of Bentis was heaven, compared to where it has found itself.

As the butterfly finished and made to go away, the spear grass started to laugh derisively, "I knew the Elephant grass would end badly, I knew it, after bragging about going to a better place and living a good life, it has ended in the bellies of the dirty cows of kush" the spear grass said.

The spear grass began to spread it's stems and brag to the carpet grass about how well it would end up.

"I will be taken to the Beverly Hills, and I will be surrounded by many expensive plants, and animals will worship me."

"You shouldn't mock the carpet grass, you should try to learn for its ordeal, and not laugh at it, let's keep our calm and composure, spear grass, everything good will come."

The spear grass looked at the carpet grass proudly, sighed, and moved away.

One day, a woman dressed in a luxuriant gown, walked past the Bentis hills, her gown was laced with silver linings and many expensive stones. The spear grass was ecstatic, "this is my time," it thought to itself, I have finally made it out of dry and drooly hill it shouted, gladly.

As the woman approached, it bent over spreading its stems to make sure the woman harvests it, when the woman came closer, she hesitated a little and finally harvested the spear grass.

The spear grass was so happy, this was the day it had been hoping for all these while, and its joy could not contain its heart.

After a couple of days, the butterfly brought the news of the fate of the spear grass to the carpet grass, "the spear grass and her children are being fed to the fodders," it said, "they eat and poop on it all day, and the spear grass wished it had remained at Bentis".

The carpet grass felt sorry for the spear grass, it wished the spear grass and the elephant grass had found a better new home than what they have.

One day a woman walked past the Bentis hill, she wore a purple chemise and leather sandals, she sang aloud as he walked, she saw the carpet grass and liked it, she uprooted the carpet grass and took it to her home, in Beverly hills.

She treated the carpet grass well, and she planted the carpet grass at Beverly hills, alongside with other precious plants. She pruned the carpet grass, the carpet grass was the lawn, her children played on the carpet lawn happily. The carpet grass interacted with other plants, the carpet grass was happy ever after.

The butterfly took the news of the carpet grass to the Elephant grass and spear grass. It kept telling the story everywhere it went to everyone who would pay attention.

Conclusion

CONCLUSION: HOW TO IMPROVE ONESELF AND OVERCOMING STRESS

We all face different challenges and hurdles at some point or the other in the course of our lives, and sometimes the pressure might just be overwhelming and hard to handle. When we feel overwhelmed, when we feel unsure about how to meet the demands and cope with the pressures placed on us, we experience stress. In little portions, stress can be a good thing. It can enact the push you need, a little motivating factor to strife for the best, and also to stay focused and alert. Stress is the factor that keeps you on your toes during a presentation in school or that force that drives you to study for your exam when you'd rather be in the cinemas. But when the going gets too tough, and life's demands exceed your natural ability to cope, stress immediately becomes a threat to both your physical and emotional well-being.

There's a biological stress response, a natural one that is meant to protect and support us. It is what helped our ancestors survive the dangerous situations they faced frequently. But in the modern world, most of the stress we feel is a response to psychological rather than physical threats. It's either we're stressed over a looming deadline, assignments, projects, work presentations, an argument with a friend, or a warehouse full of bills, the warning bells ring. And just like a caveman confronting a sabretooth tiger, we go into an automatic overdrive.

Stress is known to be a psychological and physiological response to events that upset our personal balance. When faced with a threat, whether to our physical safety or emotional equilibrium, the body's defenses kick into high gear in a rapid, automatic process known as the "fight-or-flight" response. We all know what this stress response feels like, heart pounding in the chest, muscles tensing up, breath coming faster, and every sense on red alert.

If stress were to be a disease, it would be considered a world pandemic. Stress has so much adverse effect on the human body when it's consistently experienced. In this age of technology, coupled with the fast-paced growth of all industries and sectors, we tend to push our bodies to the limits. There's the strife to achieve another milestone, another noble laureate, there's just that one more bound we want to break. And as much as this is very good and healthy for the growth of the society as a whole, so much "evil" is being done to our bodies.

We in this modern times have become masters and professionals at maintaining bad, terrible and horrible sleeping patterns, masters at unhealthy eating, we also in recent times have mastered how not to care so much about our health. Good health is very much underrated. All these form a composite of well-balanced ingredients for a meal of stress. Stress has become opium for those wanting to achieve landmarks in their lifetime.

If you have a lot of responsibilities and worries, like a demanding work, the banking sector, for instance, you may be running on stress a good portion of the time—launching into an emergency mode with every traffic jam, phone call from the office, or every shout in the neighborhood. But the problem with the stress response is that the more it is activated, the harder and harder it is to shut off. Instead of the body system to level off once the crisis has passed, the stress hormones, heart rate, and blood pressure remain elevated, all red flags. Furthermore, repeated activation of the stress response takes a heavy toll on the body. The body always needs a certain amount of time to recuperate. Just like a machine needs to be serviced from time to time to keep the systems in check and to avoid breakdown. Prolonged exposure to stress increases your risk of everything from heart disease, obesity, and infection to anxiety, depression, and memory problems. Because of the widespread damage it can cause, it's essential to learn how to deal with stress more positively and reduce its impact on your daily life.

Stress affects virtually every aspect of the human body, the mental health, the psychological health, the total well-being of the person. It affects the total output of the person. The person slowly dissipates, and if conscious efforts are not taken to check the levels of stress, such persons will fade out and eventually burn out. If, for instance, their mental health is impaired, and such a person works in a field of constant logical thinking and loads of mental processes, the person cannot function. For instance, in the battlefront, soldiers have been diagnosed with suffering from Post -Traumatic Stress Disorder upon leaving the war field. Extreme stress reactions can be birthed from sudden and catastrophic events or traumatic experiences such as natural disasters(hurricanes, tornadoes, tsunamis amongst others), sexual assaults(molestation, rape, trafficked victims), life-threatening accident(survivors of shipwrecks, like the survivors from Titanic, survivors from plane crashes) or participation in combat. After the initial shock and emotional crisis, many trauma victims gradually begin to recover from its effects. But as we know that for every case there are always exceptions, in some people, the stress symptoms never go away, the body is not able to regain its equilibrium, the distortion caused by the trauma is so great that the effect remains permanent, and life doesn't return to normal. This severe and persisting reaction to trauma is known as post-traumatic stress disorder (PTSD).

Common symptoms of PTSD include:

- Intrusive thoughts, or nightmares about the trauma
- Avoidance of places associated with the trauma
- Hyper-vigilance for signs of danger
- Chronic irritability and tension
- Depression.

PTSD is a serious disorder that requires professional intervention.

Chronic stress plunges it's fangs into your mental health, causing emotional damage in addition to physical ailments. People who have experienced varying levels of stress have been seen to have mouth ulcers, stomach ulcers amongst other ailments. Long-term stress can even rewire the brain. One might begin to act off as the mind is being consistently hammered and reshaped by stress. Over time, stress can lead to mental health problems, such as:

- Anxiety
- Depression
- Eating disorders, and
- Substance abuse.

The Body's Stress Response

The "fight-or-flight" stress response involves a cascade of biological changes that prepare us for emergency action. When our senses are alerted to danger, a small part of the brain called the hypothalamus sets off a chemical alarm. Epinephrine races through the bloodstream, readying us to either flee the scene or battle it out, and in some cases, freeze.

Heart rate and blood flow to the larger muscles increase so we can run faster and fight harder. Blood vessels which lie under the skin constrict to prevent blood loss in case of unintended injury, pupils dilate—they get bigger, so we can see better, and our blood sugar spikes, giving us an energy boost and speeding up reaction time. At the same time, processes in the body that do not aid the whole "flight-or-fight" event are suppressed, the digestive and reproductive systems, growth hormones, and the immune response are put on hold.

To get a handle on stress, one needs to learn first how to recognize it in oneself. Stress affects the mind, body, and behavior in many ways. The specific signs and symptoms of stress vary widely from person to person. Some people primarily experience physical symptoms, such as low back pain, stomach problems, and skin outbreaks. In others, the stress pattern is centered on emotional symptoms, such as crying. For some others, change in the way they think or behave predominates. It is very important to identify the symptoms one typically experiences when under stress. If the red flags are known, one can take early steps to deal with the stressful situation before it—or your emotions—spiral out of control to other complications.

After the first stage of identifying stressors, one can move to the next stage. Tackle the stress agents. Learning to be kinder to yourself, in general, can help you control the amount of pressure you feel in different situations, which can help you feel less stressed.

Learning to reward yourself for achievements – even small things. Like completing a piece of work or making a decision (even if its small). You could take a walk, read a book, and treat yourself to the food you enjoy.

Get a change of environment temporarily. You might want to go outside, or even visit a friend's place or go to a café for a break.

Take a break or holiday, sometimes away from routine work can do a lot of work in relieving stress. You'll feel less stressed when there is dynamism in one's life. Also, learn to forgive yourself when you make a mistake or when you don't achieve something you hoped for. Always have it at the back of your mind that nobody is perfect, and putting extra pressure on yourself doesn't help.

Use help from people around you. Remember that whatever you're going through that's causing you stress, you don't have to cope with it alone.

Friends and family: Sometimes talking to people close to you about how you're feeling can have a tremendous impact on stress relief.

You can also get support at work. For example, your line manager, human resources (HR) department e.t.c Do not worry that talking to your manager or colleagues about stress will be seen as a sign of weakness.

Support at university or college, such as your lecturers, student union, or student services.

The is also the online peer support. Sometimes sharing ones experience with people who have been through something similar can really go a long way in helping one to feel less alone.

The International Stress Management Association, an organization established to help those dealing with stress at various levels and degrees, can help find a specialist stress practitioner in your local area.

What treatments are there for stress?

Stress is not medically diagnosed, so there is no specific treatment for it. However, if you are finding it hard to cope with day to day activities because paranoia and one's senses are always at alert for danger and there's also a need to make everything perfect, thus heightening the stress levels a person experiences, treatment can come into play.

Talking treatments

Speaking and dialoguing with trained personnel about stress can help in stress relief therapies. One connects with his thoughts and emotions and can see things more plainly. Some talking therapies include:

Cognitive-behavioral therapy (CBT). This helps to understand one's thought patterns, recognize various trigger points, and identify positive actions that can be taken to combat stress at various degrees.

Mindfulness based stress reduction (MBSR). This combines mindfulness, meditation and yoga with a particular focus on reducing stress. This tries to cover the overall wellness of the person.

Medication

Since stress in itself is not a mental problem, there's no specific drug to use. However, your doctor might offer to prescribe:

- Sleeping pills or minor tranquilizers if you're having trouble sleeping

- Antidepressants if you're experiencing depression or anxiety

- Medication to treat any physical symptoms of stress, such as irritable bowel syndrome (IBS), or high blood pressure.

Eco-therapy

Eco-therapy is a way of improving your wellbeing and self-esteem by spending time in nature. This can include physical exercise in green spaces or taking part in a gardening or conservation project.

Complementary and alternative therapies. Asides the therapies and various ways of relieving stress named above, one can also find certain alternative therapies to help you manage feelings of stress. These might include acupuncture, aromatherapy, massage, or traditional Chinese Medicine.

The complete wellness of the body is paramount as that in itself aggregates to the total wellbeing of the society. Stress has killed people, burnt them out, and it's still doing so. But with proper knowledge on how to manage and efficiently have a balanced life amidst all the stress that we have today, one can survive for years to come.

CPSIA information can be obtained
at www.ICGtesting.com
Printed in the USA
LVHW101748090221
678844LV00007B/133